BEING HUMAN

The path to self-acceptance, resilience and happiness.
Natalie Read, PGdip Psychosynthesis Counselling

Contents

Part I – Being Human in Context

Part II – Toolkit to Overcome and Prevent Specific Difficulties

Part III – Embracing Change and Living with Happiness

CONTENTS

Introduction

THE COURAGE TO BE HUMAN

Admitting your deepest fears isn't easy – it may even feel terrifying. Maybe you're worried about being different or even abnormal. What if you have a mental health problem? Will people act differently towards you or judge you? And how long will this issue last and will you ever be free of it? You may have thoughts that make you feel ashamed and are petrified of voicing them. Something's wrong but you don't know what. Maybe you're struggling with motivation, anxiety, relationships, can't get out of bed or stop crying. Yes, all of this is hard to acknowledge to yourself, let alone someone else. Showing your 'worst' or being vulnerable in front of someone else can be excruciating. Yet, all of these things are familiar to a counsellor and my aim in writing this book is to show you that you're not so different after all.

I also want to applaud your courage in picking up this book; it takes guts to seek help and I hope you find some comfort in it. You've taken an important first step: acknowledging something to yourself and now you're doing something about it. When I first meet a new client, I'm always inspired by their courage for walking through the door and admitting that they want help. Sometimes clients expect me to be shocked or horrified by their reasons for coming. Contrary to this, I honour the risk they've taken and the trust they place in me by sharing their story. My job as a counsellor is to listen and support, not judge, and a big part of my role is normalizing experiences and helping people to realize they're not so different from others – a human being. Yes, even you – it's common to imagine you're an exception. Your fears and concerns are highly likely to be familiar to me too.

This book isn't just about overcoming mental health issues, it's also about helping to prevent them manifesting in the first place so if you're not experiencing any difficulties at present, but want to understand more about yourself, then this book is equally for you. Any work that you undertake now can help build your resilience and happiness while helping to prevent mental health difficulties from arising or limiting the extent of them. In this introduction, I share why I believe this book is needed and how it can help, and whether or not you should seek professional support.

The challenge we face

Everyone's affected by mental health difficulties at some point in their lives and that's been the case for a long time. In the UK, approximately one in four people will experience a mental health problem each year.[1] Working as a Student Counsellor for the last 12 years, I've witnessed a dramatic increase in the number and complexity of cases, as the amount of undergraduates reporting mental health concerns has risen fivefold[2] – and this trend isn't showing any signs of slowing down. These issues are regularly reported in the media and everyone seems to be talking about the mental health crisis that we face. These issues are not unique to the UK either – this is a global issue.

However, it's not just students; mental health affects all young people and it's clear that mental health issues are now affecting people earlier in their lives than in the past. A recent NHS report found that 12.8 per cent of 5–19-year-olds have at least one mental health disorder and this percentage increases with age, with 16.9 per cent of 17–19-year-olds affected.[3] These figures may well be an underestimate because not everyone affected by a mental health issue comes forward for help. Another report states that 20 per cent of adolescents are reported to experience a mental health problem in any given year.[4] It's also well known that the earlier somebody receives help, the easier it is for them to recover, yet 70 per cent of young people affected by mental health difficulties don't receive the appropriate support.[5]

Why is mental health on the increase?

We live in an increasingly complex world. Every generation faces challenges and the current ones stem partly from technologies that are meant to help. The Dalai Lama has written about 'the paradox of our age': that even though we live in a modern world of more choice, technology, fast food and so on, we also have less quality of life, peace and rest.[6] Life can feel like a constant treadmill as we try to fit in more and more into our days, and this can have a detrimental effect on our physical, mental and emotional health. Many people feel overwhelmed and out of touch with their emotions. Sometimes you might feel as though you're wearing a mask to keep up – the real you is hidden deep inside. There's constant pressure. Just thinking about it can be enough to cause a headache.

It's hard to switch off from your phone, other gadgets and social media. You can look up symptoms and then spend time worrying about an issue you may not even have. While looking for strategies to help you, you'll access both positive and negative options, and this might give rise to ideas you wouldn't have thought of otherwise. When I was at school, I didn't consider self-harm because I'd never heard of it. This wasn't down to my school but down to the fact that self-harm instances were much lower then, and I think the lack of the Internet was a factor. Now you can devote lots of time to looking things up, comparing yourself to others, staying in never-ending conversations and seeing photos of yourself that you wish you hadn't. Comparing yourself to others can impact your self-esteem. Studies on social media usage have found that too much time spent on social media sites, such as Facebook and Instagram, can lead to issues with body image and depression.[7] Instagram was rated as the worst social media platform for impacting on young people's mental health, as highlighted on an NHS website.[8]

Technology, when used appropriately, has huge benefits and it's a typical part of today's world but it also has some pitfalls. To help minimize the negative effects of too much tech, you need appropriate boundaries and time for reflection so that you can check in with yourself, relax and rest properly. It's also important to spend time alone, away from constant news reports about war, terrorism and violence, and to switch off from the world. Otherwise, it's easy to become anxious and start to believe the world is a fearful place.

There are other issues in the world today, such as financial and environmental pressures, while the job market is increasingly competitive and unpredictable. The educational curriculum seems to be bursting at the seams with more things to learn each year. Drugs, alcohol and nicotine also play their part. An article in *The Guardian* highlighted that 11–16-year-olds with a mental health disorder were more likely to have consumed drugs, alcohol or nicotine.[9]

Self-esteem is also a factor. Feeling different to others, being uncomfortable with who you are, facing difficulties and transitions, as well as comparing yourself to others, which we've already touched on, affects your confidence. Any transition, such as starting university, a new job, changing home or life events, such as death or divorce, can impact your self-esteem. So yes, it's really tough in the world right now and it's not down to you being unable to cope, as we all need support and strategies from time to time.

For this reason, I think it's helpful to see mental health as a continuum – one we all go up and down at various points in our lives. Stress, coping with life events and lifecycle changes affects everyone. Experiencing mental health difficulties can be fleeting, in response to a particular situation, or it can hang around for longer. The symptoms can also range from mild, moderate to severe. Wherever you are on the continuum, it doesn't have to be permanent. You can recover and take steps towards the other end. Everyone experiences difficulties that could be termed a 'mental health' issue, but it's not necessarily a mental health condition so they may not be stuck with it. While the experience can be distressing, no one should be ashamed or feel isolated.

Why I wrote this book

Like many people, I'm very concerned about the increasing trend of young people experiencing mental health issues and, given that resources are stretched and it can be difficult to get help quickly, I decided to write this book to provide another option of support. This book is ideally suited to anyone who wants to prevent themselves from needing support in the first place or is experiencing mild-to-moderate symptoms. For those with moderate to severe symptoms, this book may support you alongside one-to-one support, or while you are waiting for it, by helping to build resilience and positive coping strategies. I don't pretend to have all the answers or a magic pill – although that's a common request by the way – because you do have to 'work on yourself', but the more you do, the bigger the rewards. Difficulties don't tend to go away by themselves. Well, not in the long run anyway.

I've written this book as a psychoeducational handbook: it includes information about mental health and life's challenges but uses my words rather than theoretical explanation. You might even find it helpful to think of this book as a good friend; it sometimes reassures and sometimes challenges (in a supportive and respectful way) – whichever helps you best at the time. Working through the following chapters, you'll uncover any layers that might be preventing you from realizing that you're human – having good and bad experiences just like everyone else. Along the way, I'll debunk the myths and help you to strip away the assumptions and judgements so that you can see you're wonderfully human. Just as you are. Even if you don't know it yet. That might sound scary or repulsive right now but I urge you to take a risk and read this book anyway.

My personal passion is finding what brings happiness and peace to individuals. On my own personal quest, I've worked in the corporate world, trained to be a counsellor (where you have to 'work on yourself' as well as learn to help others), participated in many self-development courses and read extensively. I've explored many paths but experienced the biggest wins with mind, body, spirit approaches and so I bring a number of these ideas to this book alongside more traditional approaches. I believe in an ever-complex world; we need an ever-expanding list of options.

I've tried to bring these options to you in everyday language and it was a conversation with my brother that helped me see the importance of this. He is a very down to earth, practical person and leans more towards atheism. One day, I was talking to him about an 'alternative' concept that I believed would be helpful to him and he stopped me mid-sentence saying he couldn't 'hear me' – the language didn't resonate. I re-explained in everyday language and he not only heard the message but also agreed with it. Hopefully, reading about these new ideas in everyday language will also make sense to you.

As a counsellor, I always work with the belief system of the person in front of me because I believe that you know yourself best. As in life, you may resonate with some of the ideas and not with others. We all need to find our path: learning more about who we are, what we believe in, what works for us and making our own decisions. This isn't only an important element of counselling, but also a step towards happiness. Apply the same principle to this book. Trust yourself!

The book focuses on helping you to be more aware of yourself and what might be going on for you. As well as addressing symptoms in the short-term, the aim is to help with the long term. By building your awareness, you'll be able to work on self-acceptance, resilience, happiness and self-love, thereby helping prevent mental health difficulties from occurring or reducing the extent of them if they do.

What's in the book and how to use it

My experience as a counsellor has included one-to-one sessions, self-help programs, and facilitating workshops and groups. It's been a privilege to witness in most cases, a transformation from crisis towards a more confident and optimistic outlook. Although each individual is unique, I've increasingly noticed common themes to my sessions and I've included many of these alongside client examples of how people can be affected by life and mental health difficulties. All of these are fictional examples in order to protect client confidentiality – so they are not based on one individual but on frequently occurring narratives. I hope these examples help you to make sense of what's going on for you and, as a result, you'll hopefully feel more understood and less alone.

It can be tough enough in this world without feeling this way too.

The book's divided into three separate parts and you may find it helpful to keep a pad and pen handy, or even better, start a journal to record your answers to the exercises and your self-reflections. You can also download a printable version of some of these exercises via my website: www.natalieread.co.uk

Part I is all about our emotions, coping with life's ups and downs, true versus false happiness and how all of this makes us human. Life's much happier when you challenge any of the beliefs and judgements holding you back. In doing so, you can feel more empowered instead of feeling like a victim.

Part II is dedicated to the most common reasons why people seek help from a counsellor. What they are, how they come about and how to deal with them. I share lots of exercises to help you reduce symptoms, as well as to prevent them from reoccurring or emerging in the first place.

Part III focuses on how to build resilience, happiness and self-acceptance. How to feel more comfortable with who you are so you can cope better with difficulties and attract more positive situations. I've brought in a variety of different perspectives in addition to more traditional solutions.

How you read the book is down to you. You might choose to dip in and out of the chapters you think will be most useful but I think you'll benefit most if you read through the whole book from start to finish. Each chapter builds on the one before and there are many links between the various difficulties. I appreciate there are issues affecting young people today which I haven't gone into specifically, such as addictions and self-harm, but working with this book will help you indirectly with a broader range of mental health issues than those covered. You'll also find a list of resources where you can find more targeted help at the back of the book.

About the meditations

Meditations in the style of guided visualizations[10] support most of the chapters, although these can be used interchangeably. Where there isn't a meditation at the end of a chapter, please use any of your own choices. I have used these meditations for many years in my workshops and found they can help address and prevent mental health difficulties at a deeper level and are effective whatever your belief system. You don't have to be spiritual or religious in order to benefit, but equally, you might be. Each audio is on YouTube and you can access them by copying the links into your web browser i.e. Internet Explorer, Google Chrome, Safari etc. (You'll find a full list of links in Appendix I.)

The benefits of meditation are far-reaching and include:

- Calming the mind
- Relaxing the body
- Reducing stress and anxiety
- Increasing awareness of yourself (body sensations, emotions, thoughts)
- Increasing intuition
- Connection to a higher aspect of yourself (internal or external depending on your belief system)
- Increasing happiness
- Increasing performance and motivation
- Increasing decision-making
- Increasing confidence and self-esteem
- Improving creativity
- Enhancing health, wellbeing and the immune system
- Reducing blood pressure, slowing heart rate and breathing
- Improving sleep
- Improving relationships
- Increasing energy and focus

To get the maximum benefit from the meditations, please ensure the following:

- Find a place which is quiet, comfortable and relaxing, where you're unlikely to be disturbed. You might like to do the meditations with a friend, parent or partner to start with.
- Sit or lie with a straight back. Sometimes you feel cooler during meditation, so have an extra layer or blanket to hand.
- Prepare yourself for meditation by writing down any thoughts that might be on your mind.
- Set the intention to relax, to have a positive experience and let go (detach) from any outcome and also your perfectionist or critical self. If any thoughts do arise (it's totally natural) thank them and refocus on the meditation.
- Always start by grounding yourself first. In all of my recorded meditations, I talk about imagining the roots from a tree going into the ground, as well as branches connecting to the sun. Putting yourself in a golden ball of protection, or whatever fits your belief system, while acknowledging you're safe is also advisable. This allows you to relax into the meditation.
- Repetition of the meditations over a few days, weeks (or months) will enhance the experience and have a more beneficial effect.
- Never listen to a meditation while driving or operating machinery.
- If you feel overwhelmed, uncomfortable or your anxiety increases, please stop using the meditation.

If you're experiencing a particular trauma or emotional difficulty, meditation can bring up the feelings you might have repressed or avoided. If this is the case, I recommend trying meditation after addressing your feelings. You may wish to seek professional support to do so.

Should I see a counsellor or GP?

This book is not a substitute for professional help. If your symptoms are having a major impact on your life, or you're in crisis in any way, please seek the appropriate help. While this book may support you alongside the process, or help prevent issues from manifesting, you may prefer to talk to a professional in person. If your symptoms have presented for a long period of time or you're at risk of harm, I would advocate seeking help immediately. Further sources of support can be found at the end of this book.

How this book may benefit you

My hope is that by reading this book you'll feel more accepting of yourself and reassured that you're not alone. You'll understand more about yourself and have a healthy toolkit of options to support you and help you feel more confident and resilient. You may also begin to understand what makes you happy and how to attract more of this into your life.

Remember

The more work you do on yourself, the stronger the possibility of positive change.

There's no shame in having something to work on or needing help – we all do from time to time. As a human being, you don't have to be perfect. My life is in no way perfect either – perfect doesn't exist and I'm equally human. I hope this book helps you find more self-acceptance, resilience, happiness and self-love, and helps you to enjoy being human.

Part I

BEING HUMAN IN CONTEXT

Chapter 1

GOING WITH THE FLOW OF LIFE

I thought I'd be happy when I left university. After all, I was one of the lucky ones with a graduate job. Everyone seemed so pleased for me and that made me happy. I didn't realize at this point what I wanted in life or what actually brought me happiness. I think I knew I was a people-pleaser but didn't understand the implications of this. I was full of expectations about life. For me that meant going to university, getting a good job, being financially independent and having an active social life. I chose to work and live in a city because that was what everybody else was doing. I expected to eventually meet the man of my dreams, settle down and live happily ever after. Even though I didn't really believe in fairy tales, deep down they still had an influence. I didn't have another version of what to expect so being saved by a prince seemed like a good escape option.

Other common expectations: I'll go to university, have the time of my life and meet my best friends forever. If I'm friends with the in-crowd, I'll be really happy and my social life will be much better. When I leave home, get a partner or start a family, I'll be sorted. Life is full of these sort of assumptions. Can you recognize any of them in your life? Your assumptions are often subconscious and you may not realize their impact on you. So when things don't go to plan, you might feel deflated. As though you've failed in some way. I think everyone can resonate with one of these expectations.

What's the story that helps you out when you don't meet the prince or princess? Or when they turn out not to be quite as virtuous as in the movies? You can probably temporarily distract yourself from the disappointment that's growing deep down. Maybe everything will turn out well if I just give it a bit more time. At some point though, it's time to face the truth.

In this chapter, we'll look at the pitfalls of having expectations. How to go with the flow and have a more realistic view of life. There's a lot to unpick here but first, let me continue with my story…

When life doesn't go to plan

I thought I was happy at the time. My life was generally good. I had friends, a job with prospects and I was close to my family. Even though there was a niggling feeling of unhappiness deep down, I kept dismissing it. From the outside, it seemed as though I was living the dream… then, everything changed almost overnight.

One year after joining the company, I started to get pains in my hands and arms. It started with tingling in my fingers but then became a dull ache in my forearms. Both arms then became visibly swollen and it was hard to find a comfortable sleeping position. Everyday tasks became more difficult. I had to ask others to help me lift things. I couldn't eat my dinner without somebody cutting up the food for me. I wasn't much fun to be with because I couldn't distract myself from the pain and worry. I also felt as though I was a burden to others. I hated asking for help. Work became impossible as I couldn't write or use a computer. Even using the telephone hurt. I was diagnosed with RSI (repetitive strain injury) and advised to rest by my doctor and referred to Occupational Health.

At 22 years old, I was unable to work. I tried to rest but couldn't relax. I was beside myself. I didn't know what was wrong with me. There was lots of information about RSI out there, but not much about how to recover. I couldn't stop worrying about whether or not I'd get better. How could I continue with my work? How could I support myself financially? I felt low, frustrated, angry and had a sense of despair and hopelessness. How could I let this happen? Why me? I was in a spiralling cycle of negative thoughts and emotion. Why was everybody else happy? Why was it just me? I felt really alone. While people were really kind, I just wanted to hide away. I couldn't imagine why anyone would want to be around me. I didn't think anyone could truly understand what I was going through.

After a few months – some of the longest in my life, I did recover enough to go back to work. I needed to use a voice-activated computer and limit the amount of writing I did. I worked on my posture, did regular stretching exercises and tried not to overwork. I managed to hold down a job and progress in line with my peers. On several occasions, I had to manage repeat experiences of the same condition. Each time the symptoms were more severe and my recovery rate reduced, while the amount of writing and computer work I was able to do diminished each time.

One day, I realized I couldn't keep doing this. During my fourth episode of RSI, the symptoms were much more aggravated than usual. I feared I would never get better so I eventually resigned and moved back to my home city. This was an even bigger blow to my wellbeing. While I felt I'd made the right decision, I was overwhelmed with emotion. I kept ruminating over why it had happened and found it hard to accept. My low mood and frustration intensified.

It was almost a year before my symptoms improved and I was ashamed I'd allowed the situation to get so bad – again. I also still found it hard to ask for help. I felt guilty. I feared the future. Who would employ me? What job could I do without hurting myself? Would I ever be able to hold the children I wanted to have? Would my symptoms develop into something else? Those were scary thoughts and my lack of self-confidence was an additional side-effect. We'll return to this story but first I want to illustrate some important principles that could have helped me had I known about them at the time:

- Going with the flow
- Avoiding judgement and resistance
- Reframing difficulties

Let's explore each one of these principles in more depth.

Going with the flow

Part of my issue was my expectation about happiness and how life should be. It can be easy to be too attached to happiness, imagining that anything else is down to life going wrong. This shouldn't be happening, what's the problem? Is it me? The reality is that life is full of ups and downs. While other people may appear luckier or happier, everyone faces difficulties from time to time. The more you accept this and recognize that you're human and doing your best (even if it doesn't feel like it), the easier it is.

Difficulties in life include rejection, relationship problems, bereavements, illness and anything that's hard to cope with. Change, such as moving schools or jobs, can also bring up challenges. By understanding that no human is immune to this, you build the resilience that you need to cope. The lows are more pronounced when you fight them. If you imagine a graph of highs and lows, the dips are less likely to be as deep when you don't resist them. You accept them as part of life, don't give yourself such a hard time and move through it much more quickly.

Avoiding judgement and resistance

If you imagine your difficulties are down to your failings, you add a layer of judgement on top of your suffering. Imagine that a brick wall represents your challenge. Each judgement adds another layer of bricks. Add to this self-criticism or contempt, and you have another layer. Dwelling on why something's happened or worrying about the consequences adds more layers. These additional layers can end up making a bigger wall than the original issue itself. How much harder is that to deal with? When I was training to be a counsellor, I read somewhere that 85 per cent of our suffering is due to our resistance or judgement of it; 15 per cent is the original issue. So imagine how much easier is it to go with the flow and face just one layer of bricks?

This doesn't mean you stop feeling. I'm not saying you have to accept everything straightaway or are wrong to have emotions – that would go against being human. If you can learn to accept that you'll face difficulties then you'll move through your emotions more easily. In my example, it was natural to feel upset and frustrated, and unrealistic to imagine otherwise. If I'd acknowledged my humanness and recognized life's not always rosy, I would have spent less time feeling sorry for myself and dwelling on why it had happened to me. I would have still gone through the feelings but spotted my judgements and lessened their impact. We'll explore more about emotions in the next chapter.

These feelings are hard enough to deal with, without believing the problem is down to you. If you have to move away from your friends or a relationship ends then, of course, you'll have feelings about it. Your confidence will naturally take a dive temporarily. It's learning not to take these things personally and seeing them as a natural part of life that's key. Accept you're not perfect, life's not perfect and nor is anyone else. In doing so, you'll make the process easier for yourself.

Reframing difficulties

It also helps to look at the hidden blessings behind your challenges because it's through making mistakes and facing difficulties that you learn the most about yourself, although it isn't always possible to appreciate this when you're in the middle of it. Yet, if you can reflect on it at a later date, you might be able to spot something helpful. The more you do this, the more you'll help your perception of future issues. You may have to take a leap of faith that it's true initially. Try for yourself in the following exercise.

Exercise 1: Building Resilience[1]

Identify a past challenge or difficulty that you've faced in life so far. It's important not to choose anything too big or traumatic, and the further in the past, the easier it will be to be objective about it. If you are still very much in the situation or it feels too painful, then it will be harder to remain objective and reflect on it.

Write down your answers to the following questions:

- What difficulty did you face? You don't need to go into details because you're trying to look at it from a bigger perspective.
- What qualities did you develop or strengthen in yourself as a result of this experience? What did you learn about yourself?
- What helped you to overcome the difficulty? Who supported you, how did you support yourself, what resources did you draw on?
- When facing any difficulty in future, what action would you repeat? What would you do differently?

What did you learn from doing this exercise? Typically people recognize they're stronger than they thought and sometimes identify with being in a better place due to having faced the difficulty. They feel reassured at their resources and support, which they can draw on again in future, and realize they learned something about themselves – new skills or knowledge or changed direction. Recognition doesn't necessarily mean that you enjoyed the process but it does give you a different perspective.

Looking back at my health issue, I'm hugely grateful for it now, although I wasn't at the time, I can assure you. I recognize that without RSI, I'd probably be in a similar job but suffering even more ill health. In facing this adversity, I learned the importance of being aware of my physical body, my emotions and the connection between them. I wasn't happy in myself and my body was helping me to do something about this. I became interested in health and self-care. I learned to look after my body and listened to the signs it was giving me.

I realized I was stronger than I thought and that change was something to embrace rather than fear. I started investigating what it was that would make my life happier and more meaningful. I decided to retrain as a counsellor and here I am now. I'm much happier in my life and so grateful for this experience because I probably wouldn't have made this change otherwise. To this day, I'm still managing my RSI and occasionally have a 'flare-up' but it's generally minor. I recognize the warning signs and am able to prevent most issues. My arms stop me from overworking and keep me healthy.

I'm also much better at not judging myself or the challenges I face. I use a voice-activated computer all of the time – this book, by the way, is entirely written and edited with voice recognition software. I never would have believed it possible all those years ago. Now when something doesn't work out in my life, I believe it's the information that I need to strengthen something in myself or to move on to a different path. I don't relish it but I don't dread it either. Each difficulty I face strengthens my resilience to cope with life. We'll explore how you can recognize your level of resilience and strengthen it further in Chapter 10.

During a break-up or argument (whether with a partner or friends), you may have insights about what could help the relationship. For example, it's better to communicate about the little things before they become bigger. Or it's important to keep up with your own interests and friendships rather than putting everything into one relationship. You might understand what makes you happy and this could benefit the relationship or any future relationship. You might see the difficulty in hindsight as a positive thing that helped to strengthen the relationship, if you got back together again, or led to a healthier relationship with someone else. If you're experiencing the difficulty right now, try holding in mind that these feelings are not permanent and overcoming this situation will help you in some way that's not yet clear.

Happiness is a journey, not a destination

Let's now return to our expectations around happiness: 'I'll be happy when I get married, move home, leave home, change subjects, if I had different friends, etc.' It's all too easy to believe that when you achieve these things you'll be happy. Making a change can bring happiness but it gives a false message. Susan Jeffers talks about how we postpone our happiness for the future.[2] Imagine these goals are ladders. You imagine happiness is at the top of the ladder, but instead, you find another ladder to climb and another and another. A more successful strategy is to learn to be happy at every step of the ladder rather than postponing happiness into the future.

While you may be happier with any of these changes, your fundamental happiness isn't 'fixed'. Any issues that were preventing your happiness before still remain – whether it's self-esteem, fears about the future, unresolved difficulties, or anything else. Also, any new job or relationship can bring happiness but other emotions too. We'll explore relationships in more depth in Chapter 9. No one person or situation can make us completely happy because happiness comes from within. Working on your inner self is more effective than seeking happiness externally.

The journey towards inner happiness

The first step towards inner happiness lies in self-understanding. What makes you happy? How much time do you devote to activities that bring meaning or happiness? Here's an exercise which might help you answer these questions.

Exercise 2: Understanding what's important[3]

Be really honest with yourself and answer the following questions for you rather than what you think other people would agree with or what you think is expected of you. If you don't know the answers immediately, don't worry, simply make a note of the question and challenge yourself to find the answer in the coming weeks. It's also a good idea to reflect on your answers from time to time as they may change, so keep a note of your answers somewhere safe.

- What brings you happiness?
- What makes you laugh?
- What brings you peace?
- What makes your heart sing?
- What are you passionate about?
- What beliefs or values are important to you?

- What gives your life meaning?
- What would you like your contribution to life be?
- Consider how much time you devote to the things that make you happy and give meaning? Is it sufficient?

NB: Everyone in life has a contribution to make although sometimes it's difficult to imagine this. Don't worry if nothing comes to mind immediately. It can take time to explore. It could be a really specific answer, such as being a scientist or helping people through nutrition, or something vaguer, such as helping people or sustainability.

Has this exercise given you some insights? You may identify some changes that you could make to bring more happiness into your life. It's hard to be happy if you're never doing anything from your list. It might be that you don't yet know all the answers. If so, taking steps to discover what makes you happy would be helpful.

As well as understanding yourself and your emotions, making friends with yourself is important, as are accepting your uniqueness and diversity to others and acknowledging your humanness – strengths, opportunity areas and mistakes. We all have them. It's not realistic to have positive emotions all of the time. Being happy requires patience, trust, perseverance and self-reflection. Each of the chapters in this book provides more information on this process and the tools to do this. It's a journey in itself. The next chapter explores emotions and how to avoid repressing them as unprocessed events from the past can affect your happiness in the present.

It's important to differentiate between what makes you happy and what's expected of you. Many people wish to help others or want their parents or friends to be proud of them. This is completely natural and understandable. Yet, if pleasing others and pleasing yourself creates inner conflict, this is something to acknowledge. There's no such thing as a job, study subject or relationship that brings happiness all the time – there will always be elements that you don't like or find difficult. If this is most of the time, it'll inevitably be hard to focus or motivate yourself. You're likely to be very unhappy in yourself and this will have an impact on other areas of your life.

I've seen many people doing a course or job they fundamentally dislike. They're often depressed and rely on unhealthy coping strategies. They ask, "What's wrong with me? Can I make them happy again?" If you're doing something to please someone else against your own happiness, it's not you that needs fixing but the situation. With awareness of what you want, you have the choice to do something about it. Accepting and facing the situation is often easier than you imagine.

We often assume what would make others happy. If you actually ask your parents or friends, their response may be different to what you expect. I imagine most people want you to be happy and healthy. They don't want you to do something that makes you unhappy. I appreciate this isn't always the case for some people but maybe there are other people in your life who would support you. Sometimes you might assume the worst-case scenario and it can be helpful to acknowledge there are other possibilities.

Internal happiness attracts external happiness

Instead of external events creating happiness, it happens the other way round. If you're happy in yourself and comfortable with who you are, you're more likely to attract a happy relationship, job, etc. In other words, rather than focusing on something external, your energy and effort are much better utilized by working on yourself because it gives you a better chance of experiencing genuine happiness.

When to seek help

Always seek professional help if your symptoms are affecting you severely, over a longer period of time or if you're at risk of harm in any way.

Guided Meditation 1: The Crossroad

The Crossroad is a meditative journey to help you appreciate the hidden blessings of the past and helps you feel more resilient about the future (see the Introduction, page 19 for how to use the meditations).

natalieread.online/crossroad

Summary

- ○ Life is full of ups and downs and recognizing this as part of life can help you to cope with difficulty and change.
- ○ Trusting in the process and going with the flow is a more positive strategy than attempting to control life.
- ○ Resistance and judgement usually only serve to prolong any difficulty.
- ○ Looking back at past difficulties can help you to reframe them and so reach a greater understanding of what you might have learned from them and help you cope with similar situations in the future.
- ○ We don't live in an ideal world. Happy ever after is learning to accept life's ups and downs. We are not happy all of the time. Happiness comes from the inside rather than external sources or material goods.
- ○ Being happy and being human go hand-in-hand. In order to be happy, you need to accept your humanness – allow yourself not to be perfect and realize that nobody else is either!

Chapter 2

EMOTIONS — FRIEND OR FOE?

I can't stop crying, I feel numb. I don't know what's wrong with me. I'm not an angry person but I keep snapping at people. I don't know why I feel this way. I don't know how I feel at all or even if I have feelings. I know how I feel but how long will it last? Why is everyone happier than me?

I am moved each time I hear a client describe how they're feeling because I know how often these emotions are accompanied by distress and often fear. Sometimes clients even apologize for coming to a counselling session as they perceive their problems to be insignificant compared to others. They cite other people who are starving or coping with something more traumatic. They feel guilt or shame, imagining they'll be judged for taking somebody else's space. There's always someone worse off but thinking this doesn't help you. It only creates resistance – the additional layers we explored in the last chapter.

You may recognize these thoughts or maybe I haven't acknowledged yours yet. I hope to address your concerns in one of the following chapters. Most people feel relief when they hear their feelings are understandable and common. They realize they're not so different after all and deserve their space to share. In an ideal world, we'd all speak openly about our emotions. We would share out loud that we too face struggles from time to time. That we feel sad, angry, scared as well as happy – sometimes intermittently or for what can sometimes feel like an eternity. Everyone would then realize how similar we all are. Instead, I frequently hear, 'Why is it just me?' It's not just you, I can assure you. Every human being faces this. Despite appearances, you're not alone.

One of the challenges we face as human beings is learning to live with our feelings. Emotions inevitably feature in every counselling discussion as well as in general life. You might be struggling with too much or too little emotion, not understanding what you're feeling, wishing you felt differently or fearing judgement from others. There seems to be a myth that we can choose our emotions but in reality, we can't.

Why is it so hard to talk about how we really feel?

Why do we try so hard to avoid emotion? We can do this intentionally or without realizing it for many reasons. We live in a world that generally avoids emotional expression and while this is changing, it will take time for this to pass through generations.

If you grew up in a family where no one showed any emotion or were only allowed particular emotions, you subconsciously received a message that it's not the 'done' thing. Naturally, you learned to hide your emotions and are likely to feel very uncomfortable showing them publicly or at all. Instead, you may favour your head over your feelings (overthinking). Or you may tend to keep busy (overdoing or overworking) so there's no time for emotion. Or you may even be out of touch with your feelings altogether.

Hollywood movies and fairy tales also give the impression that we have to be happy all the time. In real life, it's natural to experience a wide range of emotions daily. Even if you appear to be alone in this, it's more likely that other people are hiding their more difficult emotions than there being something wrong with you. Social media exacerbates this further. We portray the image that we want others to see – most likely our happiest moments and what we're comfortable with. It's almost as if we imagine we'll only be liked, accepted or successful if we show this side of ourselves and ostracized if we show anything different.

It might be that in the past you showed emotion in front of others and felt judged. You probably felt belittled, shamed, ridiculed or humiliated as a result. Understandably you now expect this to happen again. You have my full sympathy here as shame is an uncomfortable feeling. Of course, you'll try to avoid experiencing it again. Or you may have been on the receiving end or witnessed emotion being expressed detrimentally, e.g. aggressive behaviour, shouting, or constant crying. In these scenarios, it probably doesn't feel safe to have or show feelings.

Emotions can feel confusing as they're connected to thoughts and can become a negative cycle. Following a simple mistake, you might tell yourself off for being stupid. This judgement of yourself (thought) leads you to feel frustrated and embarrassed with yourself. You berate yourself with thoughts that you can't get anything right or that everybody knows how stupid you are. This leads to further feelings of low mood and a lack of self-confidence. This is a cycle which can continue on and on. It's not surprising if you lose track of your emotions in this scenario.

Unhelpful coping strategies

We can also develop unhealthy coping strategies to avoid emotions. Let's explore this with an example, let's call him James.

James hasn't been feeling himself for the past few months. Over the last few weeks, it's got much worse. He feels numb and can feel almost nothing at all, like his energy has been drained away. He's struggling to get out of bed and carry out typical everyday tasks. James is struggling to find the motivation to do any work and, even if he tries, he finds it difficult to concentrate. He's lost interest in socializing. He imagines that his friends won't want to be around him when he feels like this and he can't fake feeling happy anymore. He feels alone and hates himself for being this way. On the rare occasion he does go out, he becomes embarrassed as he drinks lots and then gets upset in front of others. He can't understand what's wrong with him as he can't see a reason to feel this way. Why can't he get over it like other people seem to? His way of coping with the situation is to avoid people altogether. He's pushing away his feelings and just hoping he'll feel better tomorrow. The alcohol was an attempt to numb his feelings but as it's a depressant, it not only highlights the feeling he is trying to avoid but also amplifies it.

It takes a massive amount of courage for James to seek help. He can't bear the thought of being seen this way. If he could, James would hide away forever but now his work is starting to be affected. People are starting to notice. His sleep and appetite are affected. He doesn't like where his thoughts are headed and he just wants to stop feeling this way. He feels afraid and alone. These are difficult thoughts and feelings to have and it can be really confusing when you don't understand why or what you're going through.

Is there a magic pill?

We'll return to James again throughout this chapter. I want to acknowledge how understandable a desire it is for the feelings to just vanish. It's a common request. Like we imagine there's a magic pill to happiness. Unfortunately, you do have to face it and work with it but it may not be as bad as you think. Equally, towards the end of counselling, people can expect that now they're over the situation, they'll always feel happy. Remember back to the previous chapter?

You cannot change life's ups and downs but you can change how you react to them so the dips are less pronounced.

You feel what you feel. Emotions pass in their own time and, ironically, tend to do so more quickly when you allow them to do 'their thing'. Avoiding emotions is at best a temporary strategy. Remember that judgements and resistance only add to the problem. A better strategy is to learn to understand how you feel, work through your emotions and find healthy ways to deal with them. It can be even better when you work on self-awareness and self-acceptance of more than just your symptoms, and the tools in this chapter and subsequent chapters can help you with this.

Control or trust

After experiencing difficulties in life, it's understandable to be scared of similar situations happening in future. Who would choose to have an argument, fail at something or feel humiliated over feeling happy? Without realizing it, you may develop strategies to prevent them from happening again. As these feelings are often subconscious, we often don't evaluate their effectiveness and they can often lead to further issues, or even bring about what we're trying to prevent. On top of overthinking, overworking and overdoing, the most common forms of this are perfectionism, anxiety or controlling behaviour. As with all labels, I imagine they are continuums we all move up and down on. We're all versions of healthy/unhealthy, good mental health/mental health difficulties – we're all human.

Someone who's a perfectionist may believe if they're perfect, difficulties and 'negative' emotions can be avoided. This is understandable but unfortunately, this belief often leads to more pain rather than less. Perfection is unattainable and, as a result, sets us up for failure rather than success. In most academic subjects, you rarely hear of grades beyond

80 per cent unless it's a maths-based subject. Being human means that everyone has positive and negative characteristics, makes mistakes and experiences difficulties. Seeking perfection to avoid feeling 'negative' emotion, often creates exactly that. The cycle of perfectionism is then reinforced.

Anxiety can be the result of an attempt to control life. Subconsciously you may think that you can stop something happening if you worry about every possible scenario. Unfortunately, it's impossible to second-guess future life events or avoid emotion. Consider nature and the cycle of life. A seed grows into a beautiful flower nurtured by the elements. The flower visibly changes throughout the four seasons and eventually decomposes back into the soil. The process starts again. Humans also experience change. While anxiety is a natural emotion (as you'll discover in Chapter 6), as a strategy for controlling life, it's impossible for it to succeed. Instead of coping with anxiety from time to time, you're likely to end up contending with it most of the time – which is not a particularly beneficial swap.

Similarly, other methods of control are also flawed and may include unhelpful coping strategies, such as dysfunctional relationships, addictions, eating problems or self-harm. These may temporarily distract you from feeling any emotion but will, in the long run, create further issues. I appreciate life can be incredibly difficult and seemingly cruel at times. I believe we're all doing our best, no matter what that looks like. If you're experiencing a particularly tough or traumatic time or are finding it hard to break out of the cycle of unhelpful coping strategies, please do seek professional support.

What happens when we ignore emotion?

With all of these different scenarios, you can understand why emotions can be ignored. This can be so effective you can convince yourself that you don't have feelings. Emotion is an energy and if you ignore it, it doesn't just vanish. Instead, the emotion is repressed. Imagine a big saucepan with a lid and every unwanted feeling dumped inside it. This can work in the short term, but in the long term, with the gentle heat underneath the pan, the lid starts to feel compressed and feelings can burst out or spill over the pan. This may be represented by a flow of tears, an angry rant, an energy zapping low mood or a constant feeling of being on edge. Long term, repression can lead to depression, anxiety and uncontrollable anger outbursts. Ironically, you're less in control of your emotions when they're repressed inside you. Yet this was probably the reason for putting them in the metaphorical pan in the first place. It's more effective to work with them consciously and you're also more likely to get a better reception from others when you do.

Repressing your emotions can create confusion as you may not link the feeling to the cause. For example, you may find yourself baffled by the extent of your sadness after losing your favourite pair of jeans but the real reason could be due to unexpressed sadness from the past. Maybe a friendship came to an end, you missed out on something important or lost a family member. Losing your jeans triggers other feelings of sadness in the pan. Repression can also create physical ailments, such as aches and pains, tension, difficulty sleeping, difficulties in relationships or the use of unhealthy coping strategies. This can then create a spiral of negativity and lead to further challenges. This cycle can reinforce the belief that feelings should be avoided.

Many years ago, I heard a particularly touching example of the impact of a conversation on a four-year-old. The four-year-old's parent was talking to a friend about an article in a newspaper. The article was about the increasing age that people leave their parental home. I don't recall the details of the conversation but there was some discussion about encouraging grown-up children to leave home. Later that day the four-year-old was crying. Luckily, he was eventually able to tell his mum he was feeling sad. He thought he had to leave home as he wasn't wanted any more. He'd overheard some of the conversation but misunderstood the intent. It made me wonder how many children have internalized misunderstandings such as this. If not corrected, the emotion is likely to have been repressed. It's hard to remember and understand stories such as this, so no wonder we're often confused by our feelings.

Emotions are natural and can be helpful

All humans are affected by life events and, naturally, we have emotions in response to them. We all experience 'good' and 'bad' emotions, including happiness, joy, excitement, sadness, anger, fear, anxiety and confusion. These emotions come and go throughout our days, weeks and months. Sometimes they appear fleetingly; at other times, they last over more prolonged periods. Even celebrities and people who appear happy all the time experience a range of emotions. Someone you would define a 'happy' person also has sad moments. A person who isn't an 'angry' person gets angry occasionally. If they're not feeling it, it's likely they've either repressed it or they've done lots of work on themselves and so are less prone to 'triggers.' It's natural to feel sad after an argument or if you've had a bad day. Equally, the same situation could leave you feeling frustrated. We're all unique in the way we respond.

The irony is that when we're in touch with our emotions and open to them, life's much easier. People know where they stand, we're less likely to snap at people and we're more in tune with our own needs. The result is we understand ourselves, so make better decisions, are healthier, find more happiness and live life more fully. We can also feel more confident about dealing with future challenges and cope with change. For those of you that want some data to convince you, whilst working in the corporate world, I saw data about Emotional Intelligence (EQ) being more important than IQ in business success at a senior level. So working on yourself is good for your career prospects as well as your happiness.

Rather than being something to fear, emotions are helpful as they provide essential information. Anxiety helps to prepare us for an important event such as an exam. If you didn't feel tense and worried, you'd find it hard to motivate yourself to revise. The anxiety highlights the event is important and the associated hormones give you the energy to concentrate and focus. Anxiety also helps alert us to danger. Have you ever had the feeling that you should avoid a particular street? As a result, you probably took a different route or travelled with friends to provide more safety.

Sadness highlights you're not happy with an aspect of your life. If you're unhappy with your job, course, group of friends, relationship or the same old hobby, it might be time for a rethink. Anger also indicates that something's not right. You might feel compelled to change something and anger gives you the energy and motivation to do so. For example, you might stand up for yourself or get involved passionately in a cause that you care about, such as the environment or animal welfare. Without emotions, we wouldn't realize how things affect us. Life would actually be harder as you'd have turned off your internal guidance.

What I'm about to say may surprise you. I feel more comfortable around people who are in touch with their emotions. When someone understands themselves and can show how they feel, it's easier for me to do the same. I feel understood and less worried about any emotion arising. Whereas conversations focused on what we think we should say can get in the way of a connection with someone. Brené Brown has a TED talk and book about vulnerability which is well worth exploring. She demonstrates how the courage to be vulnerable helps personal and professional relationships.[1-2] Emotions help us to feel real, more able to appreciate life to the full and find more happiness. When we try to turn off 'negative' emotions, we turn off 'positive' ones as well.

Let's return to James. Admitting how bad he feels and talking through his problems helps to reduce the intensity of his feelings. Voicing his darkest thoughts, concerns and worries to an impartial witness reduces his burden. Realizing that it's OK and normal to experience difficulty is a huge relief. He starts to understand how his self-judgements are making the situation worse while avoiding his friends and staying in his room is only exacerbating his low mood and isolation. He's no longer involved in anything fun or meaningful, which further contributes to the low mood.

Underneath the numb feeling is often sadness, anger, loss, despair or other feelings. The person may be unaware of these feelings as they're deeply repressed and connected to historic events, such as rejection, bullying, humiliation or something traumatic. We can underestimate the impact of these things. In the case of James, he experienced a relationship break-up six months previously which he thought he was OK about. Yet underneath the surface, he realizes he was deeply hurt by the ending. This is compounded by a number of relationship issues and endings from his past, all of which have triggered low confidence and self-esteem. James had no idea these were affecting him or that they'd created a painful story about himself which had contributed to his negative outlook for the future (we'll explore more about stories and their impact in the next chapter). Bringing awareness and understanding to this has helped James to release the unresolved emotion and create more positive scenarios for the future.

What to do with feelings

It's important to take time to self-reflect. How are you feeling? Sometimes, just acknowledging the emotion is enough for the feeling to disperse. At other times, we need to process the feeling – what are your feelings highlighting, what needs work and what action could be beneficial? Having an outlet helps to prevent the feelings from building up. The outlet doesn't have to be in public or take too much time. There are many options so find something that works for you. You may already have one without realizing it, but a few good outlets for your feelings might include:

- Talking to others
- Crying
- Breathing out the emotion
- Writing or drawing your thoughts and/or feelings
- Playing music or watching movies that reflect your particular emotion
- Taking some exercise, e.g. swimming, running, kickboxing, etc.
- Walking in nature, gardening, DIY, crafts, etc.

If you judge having emotion, you probably imagine that somebody else will judge you too, which can make it difficult to share your feelings. If you decide to share your feelings, choose someone who you trust and imagine will be understanding. The process of sharing them can help you to feel less alone and also reduce the strength of what you're feeling. Remember that you're also helping others as your sharing gives them permission to do the same and helps them to feel human too in having feelings. It's important that you choose how much to share. If you don't want to talk about it but also see the pitfalls of hiding, you could say something like, 'I'm feeling a bit low today. I don't want to talk about it but could I have a hug?'

Not everyone wants to understand their feelings in depth let alone talk about them. If this is you, that's fine. Every human is different. You'll still need to find an appropriate outlet. Maybe a more physical form of expression? It doesn't have to be exercise though. It could be walking, gardening, DIY or even stretching, as long as you are acknowledging and consciously letting go of what you're holding onto emotionally. It can take time to decide what works for you. Maybe different things work in different situations.

If it's difficult to know what you're feeling, the writing exercise below may help. Once you have worked through a bit more of the book, you might like to try Meditation 10, Body Awareness Scan, in Chapter 13. Meditation can help us to tune into what we are feeling and also help to transform our attitude to our emotions.

Exercise 3: Understanding your thoughts and feelings

Write down your answers to the following questions:

- What are you feeling? (Use colours, shapes, images and words to describe them, e.g. tension in your shoulders, a feeling of butterflies feeling in your stomach, a black pointy shape in the chest area, headache, image of a bird in a cage, etc.).
- What thoughts do you have?
- What is it like to have these feelings/thoughts or to be you in this moment?
- What does your body want to do right now – run, scream, hide, kick out?
- What do you need – a hug, reassurance, a cry, to run?

Please feel free to write anything that might feel helpful. Then try to just sit for a while and get a sense of what you might be feeling. Don't worry if you can't name the specific emotion as just doing the exercise is helping you to understand yourself more. It takes practice. You could also look back on your life and identify times when you felt sad, angry, happy, etc., and identify any clues that could help you recognize any similarities with how you're feeling now.

As you're becoming more aware of your emotions, try to notice any themes or triggers. Part II of this book might also help you to make sense of your feelings but for now, it's important to remember that feelings come and go. They're not fixed. Acknowledging and naming your feelings is a big step forward in helping them to dissipate.

Distraction is only a temporary strategy

Try not to use distraction as a regular strategy. It's OK to do this occasionally if you've a deadline or you're out for the day. A useful technique is to 'park the emotion' by telling yourself that you acknowledge this emotion and that you'll come back to it later. Specify a time when you know you'll have space. The fact that you're acknowledging the emotion is the main thing. It's important to keep your promise though; otherwise, it won't work in future. The emotion will get your attention as remember it's trying to do so for a reason.

Change and significant events

Most of our emotions will come and go freely, especially if we acknowledge them. During times of change or significant difficulties, it's natural to experience difficult emotions for a longer period. This is especially true if you're coping with loss or bereavement. The length of time varies according to the person and situation, and you may need to call on additional support or increase your self-care. By recognizing this, you're normalising your experience, which will help to prevent additional layers of emotion.

When to seek help

Always seek professional help if your symptoms are affecting you severely, over a longer period of time or if you're at risk of harm in any way.

Guided Meditation 2: The Beach

Use this guided meditation to help release any physical and emotional discomforts that you are feeling, to feel more relaxed and at peace.

natalieread.online/beach

Summary

○ We all have 'good' and 'bad' emotions and this is natural, despite how other people might seem on the outside.

○ Many people find it hard to be aware of or show their emotions, but trying to ignore, suppress or control your emotions is likely to lead to further difficulties.

○ Acknowledging your emotions rather than pushing them away is healthier in the long run and can also help the emotions disperse more quickly. Remember emotions can have important information for us.

○ Identify coping strategies that can help you to express the emotion in a safe, healthy way. These new strategies will help you to feel more in control and less afraid of your emotions.

Chapter 3

LIFE IS A STORY

How often do you stop to pay attention to the dialogue in your head? I mean consciously listen to what you say to yourself and your tone. It's probably along the lines of something like this: 'You're rubbish, you're going to mess up again and then everyone will know you're a failure.' 'Everyone's out to get you – they're just pretending to like you.' 'Everyone's so much more attractive – no wonder no one wants to go out with you.' 'Life never works out for you – you wish you were more like everyone else.' 'What did you say that for?! You just made a complete idiot of yourself.' 'You're going to look stupid in today's presentation and everyone will see you're nervous. They'll see you as the fraud you are.' 'You should have worked harder. You're just lazy.' 'Why is everyone so annoying?' I could go on and on with these but I think you get the picture.

Do you recognize yourself in any of those comments? We all 'do' negative self-talk to some degree. For some people, this follows a bad day while for others, it's reality most of the time. Everyone has a mixture of positive and negative self-talk and these messages become stories. We repeat these stories over and over again and they influence how we make sense of life. How we interpret events, make sense of relationships and how we feel about the future. They affect our mood, self-esteem and confidence. They can also be self-fulfilling. If you're not expecting things to work out, they probably won't.

It's upsetting and exhausting to think like this. For some people, it can lead to depression, self-loathing and the use of unhelpful coping strategies to try to numb the pain. As this dialogue is often subconscious, you may not realize it's even there. Or if you're aware, you don't even question it. You automatically assume it's the truth. If you're reading a book and you don't like it, you stop. If you don't like the movie you're watching, you switch channels. So why don't we pay the same courtesy to this dialogue? Why put up with negative self-talk if it makes us feel rubbish? Why automatically assume it's the truth?

In this chapter, we'll give self-talk some attention. We'll become more aware of the messages and their impact. We'll explore how to give your stories a happier ending and how to make them an opportunity for empowerment so you don't feel stuck with the same old patterns. We can't stop life having ups and downs but we can change how we interpret it – our story. In doing so, we can change how we feel. This requires some investment but, hopefully, you'll agree it's worth it.[1]

Where does this dialogue come from?

We receive messages and inherit beliefs from every group we're part of, including families, friends, school, workplace, culture, religious groups and sports clubs. In the previous chapter, we saw how family experiences can influence our beliefs about emotions. We also form beliefs about who we are, how we relate to others, what job prospects we should expect and so much more. The level of influence from different sources is unique to each person. For some people, it's more family and for others, it might be more from friends or other groups. It's also likely to change at different times in our lives.

The media also plays its part. We're influenced by trends, such as what's in fashion, what we should be eating and even predictions about the housing market. If we're told there's going to be a housing price crash, our behaviour is impacted. We'll probably offer less on a property or avoid buying altogether. Whether the market drops naturally or as a result of this belief, it's hard to tell. I read an article years ago on our interpretations of beauty. It was interesting to read that in the Western world, women feel pressure to be slim whilst in some African cultures, big is better as this reflects the person's wealth. It also showed the differences in different decades in the same country and made me realize how much our perceptions are influenced by others.

These influences can be helpful when they help us to relate to others, understand what behaviour is acceptable and give us a sense of belonging to a group. The messages can also be unhelpful and bring distress. You might hear, 'Everyone in this family goes to university or into the family business.' That's difficult to hear if it's not what you want. It's hard to feel different from others. You can feel stuck in a story that you're powerless to change. As a result, I imagine that you may be feeling sad, frustrated or even disillusioned.

The beliefs we inherit from all these influences are reinforced by our interpretation of life events, such as achievements, failures, positive and negative relationships, bereavements, break-ups, illnesses and so on. These interpretations can create a positive or negative story that we tell ourselves. For example, if you've experienced some low marks or failed a driving test, you might start to believe you're a failure or unlucky. If you've felt left out or experienced any bullying, you might believe you're not likeable. The more often this is reinforced by subsequent events, the stronger this belief becomes and the more painful it can be.

Common beliefs

Here are some of the most common beliefs that become stories in our inner dialogue:

- I am good enough/I'm not good enough.

- I am likeable/lovable/I'm not likeable/lovable.
- I am capable of success/I'm rubbish/a failure.
- I trust others/I can't trust anyone.
- Life works out/it's safe/life doesn't work out/isn't safe.

As with all aspects of mental health, I like to imagine them as a continuum we're all on. If you have more times when you believe you're good enough or likeable, you're likely to feel good, confident and positive about the future. If, on the other hand, you frequently feel like you're a failure or life isn't working out, you'll experience more sadness and frustration; it hinders your confidence and perspective of the future. As most beliefs are formed subconsciously, by making them conscious, we can choose if we wish to keep them.

The world seems biased towards negative messages. The mainstream news predominantly reflects what's not okay with the world with an occasional happy story at the end. We're more comfortable with criticism than compliments. Many of the clients I've worked with cringe at any mention of their good points. Even though there's been movement in society to address this, we still seem preoccupied with doing better, achieving higher, fitting in. Whatever the origin, these subconscious beliefs perpetuate the idea that we're not good enough. It's upsetting, exhausting and demoralizing to think like this and makes it even more important to consciously examine our stories.

Now turn your attention to your stories and beliefs. If you can become more aware of them and their impact, you can work towards doing something about them.

Exercise 4: Understanding your stories and beliefs

Write down how you perceive yourself, including the stories you tell yourself and any beliefs you know of – you may identify some very easily.

If you need a bit of prompting, consider the major events of your life and the stories and beliefs you've inferred from these. You could also think about how you perceive yourself in relation to work, hobbies, friendships, relationships and any other category that might give you some information.

Ask yourself the following questions:

- What impact does this have on how you feel, your confidence and your life?
- Are there any patterns?

Your beliefs and stories can be difficult to acknowledge, especially if you're feeling unhappy in any way. It may help to know that self-awareness is the first step towards positive change and we'll be working to change these stories in the following chapters. You can also build on your self-awareness by reflecting on the events of each week. It's much easier to spot the stories when they're still fresh in your memory.

The impact of stories and beliefs

Have you ever witnessed a conversation between two people and been amazed at how they've each gone away with a completely different perspective? It can be something simple, such as the arrangements for a night out. Take a look at the following scenario between Mark and Simon. Mark thinks they're meeting up later with a group of friends outside the pub. Simon thinks they're calling for him on the way. An easy misunderstanding that could happen to anyone.

Imagine that Simon believes he's not really liked by the group. While he's waiting at home for them to show up, he starts to wonder where they are. He convinces himself that they've deliberately stood him up. This is proof they'd rather meet up without him. His thoughts start to spiral into, 'Nobody likes me, I've never been popular' and further into,

'My life's never going to be happy, I'll be alone forever.' Does this sound familiar? We're all prone to negative thinking distortions from time to time. You become so absorbed in your thoughts, you don't even doubt their truth.

The story that's emerging here is based on Simon's experiences in the past. He's found friendships difficult and fears nobody likes him. It's easy to keep reinforcing the same story. In this scenario, we don't know the truth but notice the assumptions in Simon's thinking. How the spiralling thoughts become more and more extreme and focused on the future. It's much easier to spot this when you're not 'in' it.

Simon's probably feeling a combination of sadness, anger and possibly self-loathing. Someone who holds more positive beliefs about themselves – whether naturally or from having worked on their beliefs – is less likely to interpret this scenario in the same way. They're more likely to give more plausibility to a misunderstanding or consider other options, such as something's come up or they're running late. Even if they're proved right and discover the group isn't so keen on their company, they're more likely to believe it's one of those things rather than a failing in themselves. Even if Simon's reassured by the misunderstanding, this cycle of events will reoccur if the underlying belief remains. The belief will continue to reinforce itself. We're more prone to self-limiting beliefs when we're stressed, experiencing significant change or facing difficulties.

What is the truth?

It's important to acknowledge that your stories aren't necessarily the truth. You may already realize this and be ready to make a change. Conversely, you may be wary of this statement – I get that. It feels like the truth and you may be convinced, from the evidence in front of you, that it is the truth. Please bear with me if this is the case and read on.

You've nothing to lose. Even if you're not quite ready to take a step towards something different, you might be able to in the future.

Imagine we all own a special pair of glasses that are unique to us. Through these glasses, we see the world from our own perspective. This has nothing to do with eyesight but how we interpret the world. Your perspective is shaped by your experiences, beliefs and the stories you tell yourself. Your glasses provide a reflection of how you see things but not necessarily how others do. Another person looking through their own pair of glasses at exactly the same situation may have a different perspective. Stories are not necessarily the truth but rather your perspective. One of the reasons we believe they're true is that they repeat themselves. Let's look at why this is.

How beliefs become self-fulfilling

Cognitive Behavioural Therapy (CBT) and Neuro Linguistic Programming (NLP) describe how we find evidence to support the beliefs that we hold. This is a subconscious process and so, again, we're not able to be objective. If you doubt your likeability and believe you're not good at making friends, you'll probably avoid socializing altogether. Even if you do muster the confidence to attend a party, you go into it expecting not to meet any friends. You're likely to avoid eye contact, stay in the corner, not engage in conversation and possibly leave early. You go home telling yourself, 'I told you so.' It's not much fun listening to negative self-talk all evening. You feel deflated and probably unaware of how powerful your belief is in reinforcing this.

You'll be unaware of any evidence to the contrary. Going back to your pair of glasses, you didn't spot any contradictory evidence. It's not that you didn't want to – either you weren't looking for it or you discounted it. Maybe someone tried to approach you but, because you were avoiding eye contact, you didn't notice. Someone tried to speak to you but, as you gave one-word answers, they assumed you weren't interested. Even though you desperately desire a different ending, you keep reinforcing your story.

There's an old Cherokee story pinned up on the noticeboard where I work and it goes like this: 'There are two wolves living inside us. One feeds on happy emotions such as joy, laughter, happiness and the other wolf on negative emotions such as fear, sadness and anger.' The back story to this message is that a grandfather and grandson are having a discussion. They talk about the internal battle created by the two wolves. The grandson asks who wins the battle. The wise grandfather replies that the wolf that's most frequently fed wins. In your life, which wolf do you feed most? What story is winning as a result – the one with the happy or unhappy ending? Is this how you'd like it to be or is there an opportunity for change?

So the more likeable, attractive, good enough that you feel (naturally or if you've worked on it), the more likely you'll find evidence to confirm this. You'll behave in ways that attract this and a positive cycle is created. You've upgraded your glasses to something different. The next time you face an argument, rejection or failure, the impact is less. You realize there are other possible reasons for 'I'm not good enough.'

Exercise 5: Seeing the impact of your beliefs

To see how powerful a belief can be, for the next 10 minutes, tell yourself you're having a bad day, you're not good enough, not liked by others and nothing will succeed. Interpret everything you see and experience in this way. If you make a mistake or have a misunderstanding, tell yourself it's all your fault. Please don't try this exercise if you're already feeling low. Try it when you're feeling neutral and able to be objective so that you know this isn't necessarily the truth.

- How does this feel?
- What impact does it have?
- Notice how it spirals and becomes an even bigger issue.

On a different day, do the same for 10 minutes from a positive angle. Tell yourself you're having a great day, you're liked, you deserve to do well and so on. Try to see positive reasons for anything and everything. If something doesn't quite work out, it's one of those things that happens to everybody. You're trying your best and are human.

- How does this feel?
- What impact does it have?
- Notice how this becomes a more positive spiral and can positively influence those around you. Not only do we have an impact on ourselves but also on others.

Be careful not to quit halfway through the positive part of this exercise. It's very easy to let negativity affect us and can be a habit. You might even find yourself rubbishing this exercise completely. Each time you have a negative thought, acknowledge and thank it. Remember that negativity is not a fact but rather a judgement. If you're having difficulty, try repeating this exercise after reading Chapter 7 on self-esteem and Chapter 11 on writing new stories.

Taking steps towards change

You've already taken the biggest step by becoming aware of your beliefs and stories. The next step is recognizing that you want to change and believing you can. If you believe you can't change or it won't happen, it probably won't. It doesn't mean you're not capable or that you're doomed to failure, it's simply a reflection of how powerful our beliefs can be. Before Roger Bannister ran a mile in under four minutes in 1954, nobody believed it was possible. As no one believed it, no one achieved it. Yet not long after Roger Bannister broke the world record, John Landy, a fellow rival, accomplished it too. This record has since been beaten on many occasions since. Why? Suddenly, it was believed possible.

If you need more convincing, consider the beliefs you've already changed without even realizing. Did you once believe in the tooth fairy or the Easter Bunny? Have you worked on yourself and improved anything – maybe your grades or your performance in a hobby? Have you learned things about yourself over the years? Everyone has some evidence that it's possible to change if they look for it. The first step towards making change is having awareness of the story and its underlying belief. Once you're aware, you give yourself a choice and permission to stop the pattern reinforcing itself. It's important to acknowledge that your stories aren't necessarily the truth, just what you're telling yourself.

Once you're open to change, the next step is to challenge the evidence in front of you. What possible reasons are there for it other than the story you're telling yourself. Questions you might ask:

- What bias might there be in your perspective?
- What assumptions or generalizations are you making?
- What evidence supports your belief?
- What evidence is there that this is not true?
- What other possible reasons are there?
- What would somebody who cares about you say about the situation? Are you imagining the worst-case scenario, putting yourself down or putting too much pressure on yourself?
- What advice would you give a friend in the same situation?
- What are you learning about yourself?
- What can you do that might help you feel better about the situation?

- What belief might be more empowering to hold about the situation?

Exercise 6: Challenging your story

Now you're aware of your story/stories, can you think of any similar scenarios and are there any alternatives? It might be helpful to get support from somebody else in the alternative stories/empowering beliefs column.

Example scenario	Your story	Alternative stories/empowering beliefs
Argument with parents	'I'm not appreciated, everyone blames me, nobody loves me.'	Your parents are having a bad day. There has been a misunderstanding. Something's not working in your relationship and talking about it might help. Everyone has difficulties with parents from time to time.
Wary of trusting others in relationships	'I'm not likeable/ lovable, relationships don't work out for me.'	It's natural to feel upset and experience a knock in confidence after a relationship difficulty. Previous relationships have given important information about what might be a better relationship (revisit Exercise 1 on building resilience in Chapter 1). This person isn't right for me or it's not the right timing. Relationship difficulties happen in all relationships and overcoming them helps you grow as a person and enables the relationship to become stronger/attract a healthier relationship in future.

The following exercise can help to prevent you, in the moment, from reinforcing any existing stories further, although it might take practice before it has the most effect.

Exercise 7: Reframing

If you're having a bad day and start to recognize patterns of negative thinking, the first step is to acknowledge that these stories are not necessarily the truth.

Try telling yourself: 'Situation X is making me feel (*insert your feelings*). I also have repetitive thoughts, such as (*insert your thoughts*), which makes the feeling worse. I can see the link between my thoughts and feelings. This is an understandable reaction to the situation. However, I can also recognize my reaction is greater due to the story that I'm telling myself. The story is based on past events. If I am open to it not being true, my reaction might be slightly different. Would I feel, think or do anything differently?'

It will take some time before you're able to change your thinking patterns but every time you notice this, even in hindsight, you're making a step forward. Eventually, you will 'catch yourself' in the moment and be able to create a different reality. Instead of feeling like a victim in life, that there's something wrong with you which you have no control over or are powerless to change, you'll start to feel more empowered.

What if the story is true?

Just because we can learn to recognize our stories and choose to challenge them, doesn't mean life's always rosy. Sometimes the story is true. You can't be good at everything or friends with everyone. It's better to face it and do something about it. If it's something objective, such as your grades are consistently low and you've hard evidence to show this (it's not just a one-off), it's healthy to acknowledge this. Acknowledging reality and considering options to help you is better than berating yourself and dwelling in the past. Maybe extra tuition, reading more widely, getting a different explanation or trying a different method will help. Telling yourself, 'I'm working on it and, if there is justice, my hard work will pay off,' is more helpful than telling yourself, 'I'm rubbish.' If you've reached your maximum ceiling, then praise your effort and appreciate that you have different talents.

If the story is more subjective, such as your friendliness, attractiveness, employability, then it cannot objectively be true, unless you've met everyone or experienced every job in the world. In these instances, working on liking yourself and being true to who you are can help. What kind of people or job would suit you? The later chapters in this book will help. It might also help to get fit, change your hair, gain work experience, observe and emulate people who are good at meeting friends, read up on social skills, and so on.

Being human means we all have opportunities to learn and grow. We all make mistakes. We all say or do the wrong thing. We all face rejection and hardship. This is part of life. We add to our difficulty with our judgements and stories and beliefs. It takes time and effort to understand all of the different beliefs we hold and sometimes we need support to do so. It can sometimes be much easier for somebody else to see the pattern. Try to choose just one area to focus on at a time and remember it's not about being perfect. The more you try, the more you look, the more you have an opportunity to change your story. With a little bit of effort and determination, it is possible!

I'll always remember hearing Marianne Williamson's definitions of potential on an audio talk decades ago. She described two alternatives. The first is having to jump hurdles to reach your potential – each hurdle takes you closer. The second definition is that to reach your potential you need to take away the blinkers which stop you from seeing you're already there. The work is learning to appreciate and like who you are as in this place of acceptance, you can fulfil your potential. This book is more aligned with the latter definition. We are taking away the blinkers – your hindering beliefs, unhelpful coping strategies, etc. You might find it helpful to read Chapter 7 on self-esteem, Chapter 9 on relationships and Chapter 11 on writing positive stories to explore further how you can change patterns.

When to seek help
Always seek professional help if your symptoms are affecting you severely over a longer period of time or if you're at risk of harm in any way.

Guided Meditation 3: Weeding Your Garden

This guided meditation can help you to let go of any beliefs that are no longer serving you and help you 'plant' new healthy beliefs in your life.

natalieread.online/garden

Summary

○ Your reaction to events is influenced by your interpretation of them and this impacts how you feel.

○ Your interpretations form beliefs which either empower or hinder your life as they can become self-fulfilling.

○ You can improve your level of happiness by becoming aware of these stories and beliefs.

○ Awareness gives you the choice to recognize patterns, challenge the assumptions within them and change your behaviour.

Chapter 4

UNDERSTANDING RELATIONSHIPS

We all strive to be happy. It's natural, yet we don't always go about this in the most effective way. We're influenced by external ideas of happiness, such as the number of likes on social media, the 'perfect' relationship with someone special, or the friends and parents we think we should have. This comes from stories, movies and our perception of what other people have. We yearn for these things and, in doing so, create anticipation and longing. We're focused on the destination and believe life will be OK when we get there. As we've already explored, after a while, this can become frustrating and disappointing and we might start asking ourselves: 'Why isn't it happening to me? Why am I the only one feeling like this? I'm not feeling a connection. I feel empty. Lonely. There must be something more.'

It's not down to you as a person but that's often the conclusion we draw. This creates issues of self-esteem and layers of judgement which can be incredibly painful. In this chapter, there's a further opportunity to see how easy it is to blame yourself and become distracted from what will really help. Happiness comes from within – an internal focus. Happiness is only truly effective in relationships when we're happy enough with ourselves. Meaningful connections with others require a meaningful connection to yourself. In this chapter, we'll explore why this is true. That doesn't mean we don't gain happiness from relationships – it's just that it's the icing on the cake. The icing on its own is lovely for a while but is much nicer when the cake underneath is delicious too. Being happy with yourself is the cake. A good cake that is made from quality ingredients and well baked complements the icing in a much more fulfilling way.

Relationship difficulties

Relationships of all kinds can be a source of love, joy, happiness and wellbeing. They can also be challenging and bring sadness, anger and frustration. Difficulties are natural for everyone. No one's immune to this. Remember that 'happily ever after' is part of a fairy tale rather than real life. All relationships are a learning experience, as we learn most about ourselves in our relationship to others. There's no such thing as a perfect relationship. There's no perfect way to be in a relationship. And the most successful relationships occur when we are able to be ourselves.

Many people discuss their relationship struggles in counselling. These include issues with parents, teachers, housemates, friends, colleagues and more intimate relationships. Issues include working through frustrations and conflicts, relationship endings, relationship patterns you want to change and issues around sex or sexuality. What can you do if your partner has an encounter with someone else. What's a healthy relationship? Is it safe for me to be myself? What if I never have an intimate relationship? Insecurities within relationships – do they really like me? Will this last? What if I've upset somebody? My parents favour my sibling. These are connected with the stories we explored in the previous chapter. All of this brings frustrations, sadness, fear and issues with confidence. It's hard when you feel misunderstood or believe you're the only one experiencing this.

Let's look at Molly, who's a made-up example of someone very real. Molly's been hurt on many occasions. At school, she experienced a difficult year where she fell out with her group of friends and was then excluded by them. She became the brunt of their jokes and they spread untrue rumours about her. She felt humiliated and isolated by the experience. She withdrew from everyone, feeling alone and safer without contact. Molly was angry but tried to keep this hidden. She didn't share what had happened with her family but they sensed something was wrong. She spent a lot of time in her room and snapped at them, for what frequently seemed like little things. Her parents tried talking with her but she kept shrugging them off, saying everything was fine.

Not long after this, Molly started a relationship with a boy in her class that she'd fancied for a long time. She felt excited and elated. It boosted her confidence as she felt seen by someone and part of a new group. She felt the happiest for some time. She forgot her friendship worries and thought this new relationship was the answer to her problems. She didn't need her own friends anymore. After a few months, when everything seemed to be going well, the relationship came to a sudden end. They'd had no argument. He gave no explanation and she was left dumbfounded. What had gone wrong? What did she do wrong? She felt stupid for thinking the relationship was a good thing. What was wrong with her? First her friends and now this. She couldn't look people in the eyes as she imagined they were talking about her. She felt humiliated and ashamed. She vowed from that moment on never to have a relationship again.

Molly felt sad and frustrated. She couldn't voice her feelings but just isolated herself. She started comfort eating to feel better. The initial taste was satisfying but 10 minutes later, she felt disgusted. This made her feel worse. Her confidence ebbed and her opinion of herself turned into self-loathing. She put herself down constantly and snapped at her family – both of which added to her internal self-dislike. Everyone else seemed to be happy and able to have friends and boyfriends so why couldn't she? This thought pattern led to additional low mood and a cycle of further negative thoughts and feelings.

Now years later, while Molly is much happier, these events still affect her. Molly's in a new friendship group with people she likes to hang around with; they are kind and interesting. Even though she feels more herself with this group, she can't help but worry whether they actually like her. Do they just put up with her? Sometimes she avoids going out with them and opts to stay alone. At other times, she suggests changes in their plans at the last minute. Why don't they change at hers instead of Amelia's or go to a different party? This leads to conflict as it creates a split in the group. Not everyone goes along with her plan and she feels rejected. This increases Molly's anxiety and insecurities further.

Now Molly has also met someone she wants to go out with. She initially avoided the encounter altogether but then agreed to try a relationship with Rob. She's happy but it has heightened her insecurity. Will it last? Will she get hurt? She's become overly anxious about everything, scrutinizing what she says and does. This is starting to affect her sleep as she can't switch off these thoughts. She's becoming irritable with friends and family. She's spending more and more time with Rob and less time with friends. Rob is starting to complain that he feels pressure from the relationship and wants some time out.

Molly's feeling low, anxious and doesn't know how to improve the situation. Initially, Molly used overeating and isolation as a coping mechanism. With Rob, she's trying to manage her anxiety by spending all her time with him and trying to please him. It's also common for people to use self-harm, alcohol, drugs or get involved in relationships with people who are unkind or abusive. All of these strategies try to manage the situation but only lead to further issues. We'll return to Molly throughout this chapter after exploring some further ideas about relationships.

When to seek professional help
If you're experiencing an addiction, at risk of harm or in an abusive relationship, please seek professional advice.

Understand your defences

After experiencing relationship difficulties, you may subconsciously build defence mechanisms to prevent yourself feeling pain in the future. If you've been hurt in a relationship, it can feel excruciating. You may feel low, agonize over why or how it happened and feel angry towards yourself or others. You're also likely to feel shame. Maybe you regret something you said or did or you imagine other people are judging you. Understandably, you're likely to be more guarded in the future in order to prevent experiencing the same feelings again. This is completely natural but as the defence has been created subconsciously, it doesn't always work as effectively as you'd like.

Brené Brown describes these defences as 'shame shields'.[1] We either withdraw or hide away, focus on pleasing others or use aggression. Each of these strategies is an attempt to avoid feeling shame and the painful feelings created by relationships that have broken down. You may avoid relationships altogether, vowing never to have another one. Or you over-please and are extra compliant in order to prevent a break-up. Alternatively, you snap and blame the other. You avoid closeness to prevent further hurt. Although each of these strategies attempts to avoid pain, they're limited in their effectiveness. You might avoid hurt from another but are hurting yourself by avoiding happiness, fun and contact with others; overcompensating for somebody else's happiness over your own; or being aggressive to yourself or another.

Molly sought help as she felt increasingly anxious and frustrated. She felt better acknowledging these feelings with someone who could understand where she was coming from. She realized her painful experiences of rejection led her to believe it wasn't safe to trust anyone again. She'd subconsciously created a defence mechanism to try to protect herself from future hurt. She could also see her actions were not necessarily as effective as their subconscious intent. With her friends, she was using avoidance or conflict to 'test' if they cared for her. Deep down, she hoped they'd encourage her to come out or take her side in the conflict. Each of these was an attempt to feel reassured and bolster her confidence.

With Rob, Molly saw she was over-pleasing through spending lots of time with him and doing what she thought he wanted. She hoped that in doing so, it would help the relationship to succeed. On reflection, Molly could see the limitations of these subconscious strategies. Instead of leading to reassurance and happiness, there was a huge risk of further rejection and further reinforcing her story. While the events of the past were painful, she was able to see that she wasn't necessarily the cause. There were other possibilities for why her original friendship group had split up. In hindsight, she could see she wasn't really happy with them. They weren't as kind to her as her current group of friends. She acknowledged the split had done her a favour by helping her to find more compatible friends. With her first boyfriend, she could see she hadn't done anything wrong and the break-up wasn't necessarily a reflection of her failings. Maybe it said more about him – he wasn't ready to take the relationship to the next stage, wasn't able to stand up for her or maybe they weren't compatible.

How two halves don't make a whole

In a romantic relationship, we often talk about 'my other half'. There's an illusion someone else can make you complete. It's not a helpful idea as it creates expectations and pressure. Someone else cannot make you happy, only you can do that. You might enjoy somebody's company and feel happy when you're with them but fundamentally, happiness comes from yourself. If you're unhealthily reliant on another, you're likely to become attached to the relationship continuing. This can lead to you feeling needy, jealous and insecure. This contributes to the defence mechanisms we've already explored.

Instead of two halves, it's more realistic to consider two mirrors. We saw in the last chapter how our beliefs can become self-fulfilling. If you imagine you're not good enough or not attractive, you're likely to subconsciously find a partner that reinforces this belief. You look for evidence that it's true and the belief continues. Diana Cooper describes that whatever belief we hold is mirrored back to us.[2] This works for both positive and hindering beliefs and in relationships of all kinds. If we believe we're stupid, we attract people or situations that make us feel stupid. The mirror operates as an opportunity for us to see the belief for what it is and work to change this. So if you feel you're constantly repeating the same patterns in relationships, working on the underlying belief will help you. You can most effectively attract happier relationships by working on yourself rather than just changing your partner or friend.

In Molly's case, she realized that the past relationship and friendship break-ups left her feeling not good enough and unattractive. When she was able to reflect on these scenarios, she was able to see how these endings were so painful because they reflected her belief about herself. If she didn't believe it in the first place, it wouldn't have had such an impact. By imagining this as a mirror, she realized that holding this belief would continue to be repeated as she would be focused on trying to fix it by looking for the 'perfect' partner and friends. This would continue to reinforce the idea that she was flawed. Instead, she focused her attention inwards and started building up her confidence and self-esteem. She saw that Rob and her new friends could not fix her self-esteem, as only she could do that. While there was no guarantee these relationships wouldn't end, she felt less scared. She knew if they did, her renewed confidence and self-esteem would lead to happier relationships with others anyway.

Relationships are opportunities for growth

Whether the relationship is short or long term, it can be helpful to reflect on what you're learning. If there's a difficulty in the relationship, there's an opportunity to learn something about yourself. You might like to revisit Exercise 1 on resilience in Chapter 1 to understand your relationship patterns from the past. This insight may lead to improvements in your current relationship or the realization that you need to move on. If the latter is the case, you can apply the learning: it's a chance to attract something different next time. Conversely, if you have not learned the lesson that's coming up, you're likely to face the same situation in a new relationship.

For example, when I was 13, I experienced a lot of friendship difficulties (as did many people of a similar age, I later realized) and wanted to change schools. I felt hurt and low about myself. My mother, annoyingly at the time, suggested that we wait until the end of the academic year before seriously considering a move. She felt that if I changed schools at the first sign of difficulty, I was likely to experience the same issues elsewhere. Instead of the temporary happiness caused by changing schools, I had to deal with the situation in hand. This led to me finding a different friendship group where I was much happier and 'more me'. I can also see, with the benefit of hindsight, this new friendship group helped me on the path I'm on today. On reflection, I can appreciate my mother's wisdom.

By working on her confidence and trust in others, Molly has an opportunity for a different scenario with her friends. Instead of avoiding social situations, she can be more herself and say yes to plans she would like to do. If she works on her self-esteem, she won't need to 'create' conflict as she will have more confidence that her friends like her. Instead of pleasing Rob, she can be more open about what she enjoys and more relaxed about them both spending time with others. This will take the pressure off their relationship. By being more aware of her insecurities, she can choose whether to speak about them openly or be more mindful of any strategies to manage them. She'll find out if her friends and Rob like her for who she is and if not, find those that will. Either way, it's an opportunity for more happiness.

Molly also identifies that having an outlet for her feelings would be helpful. This would stop her snapping at the people she cares about. Talking to people she trusts and having regular exercise would give her an alternative outlet to comfort eating. The more she works on how she feels about herself, the less she needs to use food and isolation as coping mechanisms.

You cannot be all things to all people

Parents, siblings and long-term partners are, in most cases, with us for a big chunk of time. While there are still challenging periods to cope with, we learn we're loved unconditionally for who we are. Even when we show stress, vulnerability and our 'worst' traits, they'll be there.

I appreciate there are exceptions and this isn't always the case for everyone. With friendships, intimate relationships and relationships with colleagues, they tend to come and go. I've found it helpful to consider relationships as being around for a reason, season or lifetime. There are often surprises as to who fits in each category. Sometimes we need to say goodbye to a relationship in order to give space for somebody new to enter. Each relationship is an opportunity to learn something about ourselves.

We cannot be friends with everybody or have everyone that we're attracted to reciprocate. At times, we'll also say something or behave in a way that offends others. Understanding this, apologizing where appropriate and learning from experiences is part of life. Sometimes we might need to work on our communication, tact and seeing the situation from another point of view.

When a good thing is too much

It's important to have balance in life, in terms of different hobbies, activities and spending time with different people. No one person can meet all of our needs. We can't get all of our fun, support, connection, encouragement and so on from just one person. It's not healthy to spend time with only one person or group. It's impossible to expect any relationship to flourish if you don't invest in time together. If you only spend time with your parents at mealtimes, you're unlikely to feel positive about your relationship. It's common to dislike your parents from time to time – this is a natural phase as you transition towards being fully independent, separate in your own right and discerning your own beliefs.

As we saw with Molly, when we meet a new partner, friendship group or start a new hobby, it can be exciting. You might be tempted to spend lots of time with them. It might be a bit like a theme park where you love a particular ride. You keep queueing for the same thing over and over. Or like a fabulous movie you want to keep watching it over and over again. That's completely understandable and natural. You're elated, enjoying the moment and you don't want it to end.

At some point, it's healthy to take a step back. If you're giving all of your attention to just one area of your life, there'll be implications for other parts of your life. Maybe your work, relationships with other friends or your relaxation time. It can also become a bit too intense if you spend too much time with one person or hobby. You become overly reliant on this for your happiness which puts pressure on that person or group. When you face any difficulty or it ends, it's harder to get support or move on. To help you further with this, see Chapter 14 on creating more balance and healthy routines.

All relationships have two sides

When we feel hurt by someone, we naturally apportion blame to the other party. How could they do this to us? They're a really nasty person. This is an understandable reaction but it keeps us in 'victim' mode, powerless to change anything. We can improve the situation and feel more empowered by understanding our 'part' in the dynamic. This doesn't mean their behaviour is acceptable or we shouldn't address the issue though. Through awareness of the whole picture, we can learn the lessons being presented to us and help to avoid the situation repeating itself. Remember the mirror – what's the lesson being learned?

Let's explore this through the eyes of Rob. If Molly's trying hard to please him, she's likely to be sensitive to any conflict. Each time they face any difficulty in their relationship (completely normal and inevitable), Molly's likely to be fearful and try to avoid the conflict at all costs. She overcompensates by over-pleasing and sometimes by avoiding situations altogether. Rob perceives this behaviour as aloof and submissive. He finds it irritating that she never says what she wants to do and tries too hard. As a result, he sometimes gets angry with the situation. This creates an argument. Molly then works even harder to avoid further conflict. Rob is infuriated further and so the cycle continues. Her attempt to avoid conflict actually leads to further relationship difficulty.

If you can recognize your behaviour isn't helping the dynamic, you have the choice to make changes. This doesn't mean it's OK to treat you this way or that it's your fault, but it helps you to recognize what you can do to improve the situation. If you learn to stand up for yourself, people will learn to respect your boundaries. By working on your insecurities underneath the fear of conflict, you'll be less afraid of conflict arising. Often the aggressor is actually insecure or experiencing difficulties in other aspects of their life. Recognizing that their behaviour reflects on them rather than you is hopefully confidence boosting. Instead of feeling a victim to the same patterns, there's an opportunity to empower yourself and make changes.

If Molly and Rob could openly and calmly talk about their feelings and own 'their part' in the dynamic, it is likely their relationship would be stronger and healthier. See Chapter 9 on relationships for more information on this. Otherwise unspoken blame and avoidance of responsibility build both frustration and anger, and allow the situation to be repeated. Taking responsibility and learning from your mistakes and difficult times will help you and your relationships feel happier.

Remembering the impact of your stories

Your expectations and judgements also affect your relationships. Every day, we have simple encounters which result in us making either a positive or negative judgment. For example, your partner/housemate/brother leaves the house in a complete mess again. You come home after a tough day and are looking forward to relaxing. When you arrive home, you spend 10 minutes tidying up just so that you can sit down. It's the last thing you need and it's the third day in a row. Why didn't they tidy up? You feel frustrated, angry and decide they can't really care about you. If they did, they would've tidied up. You've told them many times before and you're sick of their excuses. A completely understandable reaction to a frustrating situation.

Years ago, I read an article about intentions. The article concluded that in almost all cases, intentions are positive. It's rare that someone intends to hurt you or frustrate you. We assume intention based on our perceived outcome. If you're upset by a situation (your outcome), you're more likely to infer a negative intention and vice versa. With our own behaviour, we know we've good intentions and assume that other people can see them too. If you leave the house in a mess, you tell yourself you're in a rush and will do it later. It's no big deal. You don't mean to upset anyone and assume others will understand this. Yet the recipient of the mess (perceiving the outcome as not nice to come home to) is more likely to assume a negative intention. The mess maker is lazy or inconsiderate. So there's a gap between our perceived intention of our self and others.

We also perceive situations based on our stories and beliefs. Your assumptions influence your perceived intentions. If you believe people let you down, you'll see the mess as evidence that you're right. It's hard to consider other possibilities. You're likely to be frustrated next time you see them. After a long day, who wouldn't be? Yet, if you were aware of your assumptions, you might not feel so aggrieved. You're frustrated by a messy house rather than frustrated by a messy house and nobody caring about you. The emotional impact is reduced. You're also likely to have a much more productive conversation about it and prevent it from escalating into something bigger.

So next time you perceive something negative, try to catch yourself and look for the alternative positive reasons. Try to give the other person the benefit of the doubt. When someone snaps at you, maybe it's because they've had a bad day, didn't get enough sleep or are feeling stressed rather than it being anything to do with you. They may also be making assumptions about your intentions.

Exercise 8: Understanding your relationships

Think about the key relationships in your life and write down each of the individuals. Identify the following for each of them:

- What do you admire in the person? What does this mirror in you?
- What irritates you about the person? What does this mirror in you?
- What are the strengths of the relationship?
- What could be improved?
- What patterns can you identify in this relationship that are common to other relationships?
- What part do you contribute to this pattern?
- What are your defences and how do they play out in your relationships?
- Which of your stories are showing up in this relationship? You may need to refer to Chapter 3 again to answer this question.

Notice if there are any insights or suggestions to improve the relationship (see also Chapter 9 for further ideas of how to do so).

Healthy relationships

Healthy relationships have equality, respect, give or take, acceptance of difference, and both parties will show interest in the other person. Trust and integrity are paramount as is the ability to say sorry. There's no such thing as one person who can be all things to you, i.e. meet all your needs, such as having fun, being cared for, getting help with your aspirations, getting on with all of your friends and family, etc. However, a sufficient level of support, rapport and time spent together is important. It's helpful if both people have other sources of support and interests in their life, and an outlet for venting their feelings. While venting frustrations at the people you care about is only natural, this should not be frequent or exclusive. While all relationships have occasional difficulties or a phase, overall, you should have more happy times than not.

Relationships that are harmonious all of the time only exist in our imagination. Within a healthy relationship, you can cope with, and learn from, mistakes and disagreements. The relationship evolves and grows. There's good communication and clear boundaries – having healthy boundaries means you can say this is OK or not OK. We're all different and so they may differ from person to person. It might be you expect somebody to call you if they can't meet or that Wednesday nights are always off-limits due to your long-term hobby. Being able to communicate your needs and boundaries is important.

A healthy relationship starts with you having a healthy relationship with yourself. As we've explored, the more work you do on yourself – so that you feel happy in yourself, are self-confident, aware of your patterns and have healthy routines – the better you'll feel in a relationship. There's a strong correlation between the two. Working through the chapters in this book is a good start towards this journey. You're human and naturally have strengths and opportunity areas. You'll also make mistakes and have regrets. Remember it's in your relationships where you learn most about yourself, and there's always something to learn (see also Chapter 9 on improving relationships).

When to seek help
Always seek professional help if your symptoms are affecting you severely over a longer period of time or if you're at risk of harm in any way. Also, if you are experiencing any physical or mental abuse.

Summary

- There's no such thing as a perfect relationship. All relationships have their ups and downs, and sometimes end, but you can learn more about yourself from understanding your relationships.
- Understanding what makes a healthy relationship is important and includes having boundaries, good communication and a healthy life balance.
- You can improve your relationships by understanding your defences, working on what 'comes up' in your relationships and working to create your own happiness, which is not dependent on having a particular relationship with another person.
- Happiness comes from within so any steps that you take towards this by working on yourself will not only improve your own sense of happiness but also your relationships.

Part II

TOOLKIT TO OVERCOME AND PREVENT SPECIFIC DIFFICULTIES

Chapter 5

OVERCOMING DEPRESSION AND LOW MOOD

Many people are wary of depression. You might dread the thought of getting it in the first place or hope you're immune to it. If you've experienced depression, you worry that it might become permanent or you'll get it again. These sentiments are understandable. Depression is one of the most common mental health issues in the UK. Symptoms of low mood and depression are in the top three reasons why people seek help from a counsellor. An increasing number of people are receiving a diagnosis of depression from their doctor or through self-diagnosis. It's good there's so much awareness and information, yet I believe the terms 'depression' and/or 'low mood' are often misunderstood. In this chapter, we'll explore what's normal, when to seek help, what makes it worse and what helps. My hope is that you'll feel more reassured and not alone.

Symptoms of depression

Depression can be all-encompassing; a bit like a fog that you can't see a way through. Common symptoms include low mood, sadness, hopelessness, frustration or no feeling at all –

just numb. This often comes with sleep issues, low appetite, low energy, loss of libido and it can also affect your ability to work, your relationships and your outlook on life. It's common to feel alone, despair and a sense of powerlessness. All of this is incredibly difficult to experience – especially if you don't know why you're experiencing it or how long it will last.

Let's take the case of Mary. For the past month, Mary has found it difficult to get out of bed. She just wants to sleep and hide under her duvet. If she does force herself to get up, she can't concentrate on any work. Even when she persists with work, she starts to daydream. She's got an important deadline coming up but just can't motivate herself. It's a struggle to eat anything as she's lost her appetite. She feels nauseous at the thought of eating. She doesn't want to go out, see anyone and is avoiding any contact with others. She feels numb and low in energy. She usually plays football, enjoys dance and loves playing the piano but has no interest in any of these things at the moment.

It's easy to see why Mary has concluded she has depression. Her symptoms are certainly consistent with this. She cannot see any reason for her symptoms. Everything's going well in all aspects of her life. Her work is going well, she's got good relationships with family and friends, a long-term partner and she feels happy with who she is. She has plans for her future and ordinarily enjoys a good social life. Depression feels like something that's happened to her without any explanation. She feels powerless to do anything about it. She doesn't understand why she has it or how to get rid of it. She just wants it to go away so that she can have her life back.

These are common sentiments. Nobody wants to feel this way. You can feel disempowered and out of control. It's hard to recognize yourself. We'll return to Mary soon but let's now understand more about low mood and depression.

Low mood is a natural emotion

As human beings, we all experience low mood. We naturally have daily fluctuations in mood. We might feel happy, sad, anxious and angry all on the same day. Sometimes there's no apparent reason. At other times, we experience low mood as a reaction to a situation. This might include a bereavement, relationship difficulties and endings, stress, failure and ill-health. Low mood can also be a side-effect of low self-esteem or life-cycle changes.

If something's happened in your day, you might experience low mood for a short period. Maybe someone or something upset you or you're feeling overwhelmed or stressed. It's understandable you might feel low in response to this. Sometimes the low mood hangs around for longer. This naturally affects other areas of life and it can become cumulative. This is likely to be the case when you're experiencing periods of difficulties rather than an isolated event. You might be in the process of change or an aspect of your life isn't working out as you had hoped. When low mood becomes persistent over a longer phase, it can become a period of depression. Having a period of depression doesn't necessarily mean you have a mental health difficulty though. Depression can be a response to life events such as a bereavement, ending or coming to terms with anything difficult. There are no hard and fast rules as we're all unique.

Depression helps us to adapt and change

When we feel sad or low, it's helpful to recognize that something is amiss. It alerts us to a change that's needed, a conversation that would be helpful or highlights that working on ourselves could be beneficial. Acknowledging the emotion and reflecting on this helps us to realize any important action we could take.

Not all situations are resolvable. It might be you're experiencing a period of change, such as moving home, and it will take time to put in place the friendships, the hobbies and interests and support systems that you had with your old life. Accepting you'll naturally feel sad as part of this process can help. It's prudent to take extra care of yourself and seek additional support. You might need extra outlets for your emotions while you're going through this period of change. Although it may not feel like it at the time, but at some point, when you have adapted to the situation, you're likely to look back on the period of sadness differently.

Sometimes we have to come to terms with something we don't want to accept. This can be extremely difficult. For example, an illness that is affecting you or another, redundancy, a break-up or a bereavement. It's natural you'll feel low mood as well as a whole host of other feelings. You're likely to be shocked and want to forget or believe this is happening. It can be a long process to make sense of the situation and work towards acceptance. Everybody's unique in how and for how long this affects them. Having support for this process is important.

How low mood builds up

In Chapter 2 we looked at what happens when we ignore emotion through a metaphor of a pan. If you're unaware of your feelings or find it difficult to accept them, they collect inside this pan. Over the long term, the pan lid starts to feel compressed. Feelings either burst out uncontrollably or spill over the top. Trying to keep the lid on requires energy – it can be exhausting. This combined with gently seeping emotion (the contents spilling over) can be akin to the feelings of depression.

Depression can feel confusing as there may be many different feelings inside the saucepan. Unexpressed grief, sadness or anger are the most common. Sometimes, it's a combination which makes it even harder to decipher. The spilling over often happens at a time unconnected to when the feelings were added to the pan. Several months or years later, you feel low but can't understand why. There's no obvious reason. You're aware of your past and believe you've coped with it all. Yet, experiencing little or no emotion after facing difficulties may mean the feelings were repressed inside. These stored emotions can surface when you're reminded of the past or experience something similar in the present.

Subconsciously feeling numb may be preferable to feeling these other emotions. Subconsciously, they're in the pan because you want to avoid them. They may appear scary or confusing. You want to avoid the pain of feeling them or it may be connected to your beliefs about having emotions. This is common and understandable. We all repress feelings to some degree. It's often the denial, avoidance and repression of the feelings that turn a period of natural low mood into depression.

During counselling sessions with Mary, we explored her experience of childhood. She lost her father when she was three years old. She can't really remember much about it as she was so young. She feels close to her mum and stepdad. Her mum remarried when she was five and her stepfather is kind and supportive. She believes she has come to terms with the loss of her dad as she hasn't really known any different. She doesn't remember much about her dad and can't understand how this could be connected to how she's feeling at the moment.

After further exploration, Mary recognises her acceptance of her father's loss is at a surface level. Underneath there is unexpressed grief. Her stepfather had a cancer scare recently and this brought home the reminder that life is precious. She was understandably upset and anxious about the news. While she doesn't remember her dad being unwell, she recognizes that her feelings for her stepfather may be similar to those she had felt for her dad. She's also about to leave university, which is exciting, but it also feels unfamiliar and unknown. Becoming financially independent, doing a 'grown-up' job and leaving the relative safety of academia feels a bit daunting. She's becoming the age where her mum met her dad. These events have triggered her grief to surface. As a three-year-old, it would have been hard to understand. Even though her mum did all she could to help her with this at the time, there was a hole created in her life.

Mary's able to acknowledge this grief. It feels like a black hole in her heart, containing many feelings, including sadness, loss, despair, anger and fear. There's loss at not being able to remember her dad. She would love to remember a hug or the way he smiled. There's loss for the life that she missed out on with him – the missed birthdays and school performances. The future ones they will never share. She also grieves the premature end of her childhood. She lost a part of her innocence and happiness when she lost her dad. There's sadness and anger at the unfairness of him being taken away so young. He was a good man – how can life be so cruel? She feels frustrated and angry about this. There's also fear that she could lose her stepfather or another loved one in future. What if her partner dies when she has a young child? All of these feelings were buried deep inside Mary's pan. She got so used to them that she didn't realize they were there. Any unresolved feelings can be put into the pan – anything that felt too painful to experience at the time. It's not always that you didn't want to experience these feelings, maybe you just didn't know how to.

What makes depression worse?

If you don't know what the feeling is or you don't like it, you may naturally resist it and think, 'Why am I feeling this? How long will it be here? What does it mean? What's going to happen to my relationships or work if this carries on?' These are natural thoughts and judgements which, as I've already described, can prolong the issue – like additional layers of bricks on top of the original problem. Remember, thoughts are not necessarily the truth. Each thought leads to further low feeling, then more negative thoughts, and more low feeling, and so on, which only serves to create a cycle of diminishing returns. The stories you tell yourself compound the cycle further. You start telling yourself, 'Sort it out – what's wrong with you? Everyone else can get it together. You're just a loser. You're not good enough/likeable...' In addition to this, you may stop seeing friends, doing the things you enjoy and not taking care of yourself. You feel isolated and even more different from others.

These sentiments can easily become a fait accompli. You're always going to feel like this. It's never going to get any better. You're going to lose all your friends. You'll never be happy. Nobody else is like this – it's just you. Low mood becomes an alien part of you that you want to get rid of. You don't want to feel this pain. You focus on the symptoms in the hope they'll go away. Subconsciously, you're affirming the idea that you're flawed, not good enough, a rogue human, different to others. This only adds to the problem because what we resist persists.

Unhealthy coping strategies and suicidal thoughts

To avoid or numb your feelings, you may seek out unhealthy coping strategies. For example, you may use drugs or alcohol to temporarily escape from the feelings. Momentarily, you might feel some relief but as alcohol is a depressant, it can make your low mood spiral further. It's not uncommon for people to become inconsolable after drinking. Drugs also add to further and deeper bouts of low mood in the comedown period. While unhealthy coping strategies may be positively intended, they contribute further to the issue. If you recognize you're using any strategies to escape your feelings, seeking professional help can help you to find the root cause and alternative healthier coping strategies.

When someone feels they're going to be stuck with the feeling forever, it can lead to despair and hopelessness. You might feel powerless to do anything about your situation. You don't understand your mood – why you're feeling this way or how long it will last. You might not see an end to it. Someone who has just experienced a huge disappointment, embarrassment or rejection, can feel such intense feelings; these can be unbearable and, in that moment, it's hard to imagine they will ever pass. You can convince yourself that everyone will judge you, nobody cares about you, and in this place, it feels like the truth. You want to stop feeling like this. This can lead to suicidal thoughts. This can be a really scary, lonely dark place to be in. While it can be hard to see beyond this place, it can help to acknowledge that:

- You're feeling something in response to a situation, event, perception, story (this might be specific or you may not realize the connection).
- Thoughts and perceptions are not necessarily the truth, no matter how much you might believe them.
- Feelings come and go. What you feel now, may not be what you will feel in the future. Even if you've felt depressed for some time, it's not necessarily a fact that you'll always feel this way.

- Always give yourself time. Intense feelings can come on spontaneously. It's hard to see anything positive when you're experiencing this. You don't have to make any decisions right now. Give yourself an opportunity to speak to someone, take some time and explore from a more objective place.
- Contact your doctor if you have thought of any plans to act on your suicidal thoughts. If you intend to act on them, contact your GP for a same day appointment or go straight to A&E.
- Seek help from someone who can help you to make sense of what you're experiencing and find a way through it. If you've never sought help before, then you've never given yourself an opportunity to try something different. If you've sought help and it's not worked, a different time or person might produce a different response.
- Identify someone you care about who you can contact to let them know how you're feeling. If you're worried about talking to someone who knows you, contact a professional service, such as the Samaritans (see the Resources at the back of this book).
- Distract yourself from this intense feeling while you wait for support. Take some exercise, watch a feelgood film or one you usually enjoy, listen to music, spend time with friends, etc. Break the cycle of negative thoughts and feelings.
- Remove any possible ways of harming yourself, including sharp objects, medication, alcohol, drugs, etc.
- Avoid Internet sites promoting self-harm and suicide, as well as other less healthy coping strategies. Avoid social media, the news and anything else that may exacerbate your mood.
- When you're not experiencing the intense emotion, try challenging your story by using Exercise 6 in Chapter 3 and Exercise 24 in Chapter 10 to help you find a way

forward. Also, identify the stories you're telling yourself (Chapter 3) and consider what makes you happy by doing Exercise 2 in Chapter 1. Just identifying one thing you could do that might help change the situation can help you to feel positive.

- List all the people who care about you and all that you would want from your life. Even if you can't see it at the moment, remind yourself of a time when you did feel that. You are more than your feelings at any given moment.

Seek professional help
Always seek the help of a professional, if you are, or know someone who is, at risk of harm.

What helps depression and low mood?

As we explored in Chapter 2, you ideally need to acknowledge any feelings of low mood as they arise, as this prevents them from entering the pan in the first place. Acknowledgement may be enough or you may need to explore what's coming up and find a safe outlet to express the feelings. Awareness of your feelings and acceptance of them is a prerequisite for this process to work. If you don't have this awareness, it's hard to make sense of the low mood.

It's the denial, avoidance and repression of the feelings that often turn a period of low mood into a depression. If you understand feelings are normal and happen to everyone, you'll be more able to self-reflect on them. By acknowledging the emotion, you're moving closer to accepting the situation. It's much easier to deal with something when you're not pushing it away. You're allowing the emotion to alert you to its reason for being.

By accepting the emotion and working with it, it becomes a much more manageable size, relatively, to deal with than when you add layers of bricks through judgements and resistance. Working on your beliefs about emotions and life, your stories and all of the information in the chapter so far will help you to feel readier to face any difficult situation. Although you may feel more in control and safer with the lid on the pan, it's worth knowing the opposite is usually true, as you prevent unexpected outbursts. For the remainder of the chapter, we'll explore healthy coping strategies to help with low mood and depression.

Find an outlet

Utilising an outlet for your feelings can help you to release the feelings and reduce the pressure in the saucepan. Often, the fear of the emotion is greater than the reality. I appreciate that you're taking my word for this and so if you need help to do this, it's advisable to seek help from someone who can help you. Sometimes people need support to work through their defences before they're able to process any feelings. If talking is the worst thing you can imagine, remember the alternative outlets we discussed in Chapter 2.

Exercise has been demonstrated to help alleviate depression. Not only does this release endorphins to help you feel better, it also helps alleviate the stress hormones (see also Chapter 6). You can help this by consciously imagining the feeling inside (even if they're not named) being released through the exercise. You can do this in the gym, when you're swimming, kicking a ball, using a racquet, running, or any other sport you prefer, Just imagine that as you breathe out or come into contact with the ball/ racquet, the emotion is leaving you. If you've no energy left whatsoever, you can just use your out breath to do this. You may also like to imagine that there's a big flame transmuting any energy released if you don't like the idea of it just going somewhere else.

Be around nature

There are numerous studies about the importance of nature, gardening and fresh air in helping people with depression.[1-4] Nurturing a plant or animal can also help you to feel good about yourself. You can volunteer to walk dogs if it's not feasible for you to have one yourself. Noticing all the wonders of the world through all your senses can also take you out of the feeling of depression. So whether you like walking, gardening, running, meditation or sitting on the grass, try it today, even if it's just 5 minutes. Also try noticing all of the beauty in the world, e.g. observe nature, create a list of what you are grateful for in the world.

Make time for activities you enjoy

As we identified in Exercise 2 (on understanding what's important to you) in Chapter 1, it's important to allow time for enjoyment. Anything that makes you feel joyful, makes you laugh, relieves stress and provides a sense of peace or meaning is imperative. When someone is depressed, they don't typically feel like doing any of these things. As we saw with Mary, she avoided her usual hobbies. While you may not feel like doing these things, it can add to the issue in the long term and it becomes a vicious circle. Try encouraging yourself to participate, even if it means just spending time in the company of people who care about you. You could even ask them to help you. Remember that by showing your more 'difficult' feelings to others, you give them permission to do the same. It also helps you to feel less alone. It's important to have balance and enjoyment to help counteract the more difficult feelings. You realize that you're 'more than' your depression.

Take good care of yourself

It's even more important to eat healthily, sleep well and exercise when you're not feeling your best. Typically you might want to reach for junk food or stay up watching movies. We're all human and do this from time to time. If this becomes a regular habit, it can make you feel worse. There are studies about the importance of B vitamins in helping depression and stress but you'll need to research this yourself and understand the appropriate amounts. There's also some alternative information in a book called *Medical Medium*, which if it calls to you, might be worth a read. See the references at the end. Similarly, allowing yourself to have good rest is important. The process of being kind to yourself, giving yourself a break or doing something nice is a way of showing self-compassion which will also help you to feel better about yourself.

Mary finds talking enables her to become more aware of herself and feelings. Through the process of talking, she's able to acknowledge and release much of the stored emotion. She starts talking about her dad with her family to alleviate the gaps in her memory and understand more of the circumstances surrounding his death. She writes a letter to her dad of all the things she wished she could say to him. She establishes a ritual each month where she lights a candle and spends time alone thinking of her dad. She honours his memory and expresses what she wishes to tell him. She feels closer to him and notices her black hole feels different. She starts seeing her friends and enjoying all of her activities again. She's open with her friends about how she's feeling and they offer lots of support to her. Mary feels differently about the depression now that she understands more about it. She realizes the importance of being aware of her feelings and having an outlet for them.

When to seek help

Always seek professional help if your symptoms are affecting you severely over a longer period of time or if you're at risk of harm in any way.

Guided Meditation 4: The Healing Flame

This guided meditation will help you send positive energy to difficult situations and emotions that you've experienced in the past and are experiencing in the present. It will also help you to become more resilient in dealing with future situations.

natalieread.online/flame

Summary

○ Experiencing low mood or a period of depression is often a typical response to life's events and can be very short in duration or last for a period of time.

○ Ignoring the feelings can create further issues and lead to unhealthy coping strategies.

○ Acknowledging it's OK and only natural to feel the emotion you're experiencing – for example, grief, anger, loss, sadness – and then finding a comfortable way to express the emotion often allows the feeling to pass. Sometimes you may also need to make some changes in your life in response to how you're feeling.

○ Spending time in nature, doing exercise, spending time on activities you enjoy and looking after yourself can all help to alleviate and prevent low mood and depression.

○ If your depression has been going on for a long period, you have suicidal thoughts or it is affecting you and your life in a significant way, seek the support of a counsellor, teacher or doctor as soon as possible. It's important to seek support, particularly if you feel at risk of harm in any way.

Chapter 6

REDUCING ANXIETY

Experiencing anxiety from time to time is part of being human – anxiety is a normal and vital emotion. Yet sometimes it becomes overwhelming and we start to think, 'What if I fail? What if I'll always feel this way? What if I'm always on my own? What if my friends don't like me? What if that bad thing happens?' These thoughts can play over and over like you're stuck on the same song. This is particularly excruciating if you wake up in the night and start thinking about something as it can feel even more intense. Going over and over the same scenario can be exhausting, upsetting and sometimes unbearable. The thoughts start to spiral into more far-fetched scenarios. As well as impacting on your emotions, these anxious thoughts can also affect you physically.

Anxiety is one of the most common reasons why people seek help from a counsellor. From my experience, anxiety seems to be on the rise. I believe this is connected to all of the factors previously mentioned, such as 24/7 technology – it's hard to switch off from news stories, such as terrorism, war and political unrest. There is also constant comparison to others through social media and demanding expectations from education, parents and societal pressures. We're all unique when it comes to what affects us most. It's understandable that we strive to avoid painful situations happening and anxiety can be an attempt to do this. Subconsciously you might believe worrying about everything will prevent it happening. Unfortunately, this isn't a fool-proof strategy and may create additional low mood, low self-esteem and frustration.

In this chapter, we'll explore how anxiety affects us and sometimes spirals out of control. We naturally tend to fight anxiety and fear with more fear. We judge it, try to resist it and want to push it away. This makes it worse because, as you now know, what we resist persists. It's a bit like an itch that you want to scratch. Itching it brings little comfort as you end up with an even greater itch. We'll explore an alternative way of working with anxiety by finding peace in Chapter 13. First though, we need to understand anxiety so that we can help it to work more for us and reduce the overwhelming symptoms. This is the focus of this chapter.

Understanding the fight-or-flight response

Understanding your body's reaction to fear is important. The fight-or-flight response gets activated whenever you feel stressed or question your ability to cope with something. Maybe you feel short of time, are about to face something important or feel under threat. You may be triggered by something from the past such as fear of rejection. You may fear shame or another difficult emotion. It may not even be a real danger but the thought of it. Your thoughts are very powerful and just mentioning the word failure can be enough to trigger some anxiety. Or it might be a leftover feeling you experience after discussing something upsetting in the world, such as climate change or child poverty.

All of these situations trigger the sympathetic nervous system to release the stress hormones adrenaline, noradrenaline and cortisol. As a result, your heart rate and blood pressure increase. Your breathing quickens and you may feel short of breath. Your stomach may feel unsettled, as if you have butterflies, or feel nauseous, and you may need to go to the toilet more frequently. Blood is sent to your muscles to help you move quickly. Your senses are heightened to possible danger. Anxiety can further affect your sleep, digestion and appetite. You might also get muscle tension and your immune system can be affected. Do you recognize any of these signs?

Going back to the time of our ancestral cavemen and women, this fight-or-flight response was imperative in the face of predatory animals (and our bodies respond in very much the same way now as they did then). The hormones prepared the body to either run away from or fight the danger, and so increased the chances of survival. The physical act of running or fighting utilized the hormones so the body returned to balance once the danger had passed.

Anxiety in the modern world

Whereas facing a wild animal is a real scenario, modern-day situations can be real or imagined. In cavemen times, fight or flight probably happened much less than it does in our modern world. These days, the stress response can be activated repeatedly throughout the day. Possibly several times in a matter of minutes: 'Will I ever get this done? I'm going to be late. What did I say that for? What's going to happen in the future?' Meeting deadlines, juggling priorities and imagined situations, irrespective of how likely they are – for example, fear of failure or what somebody *might* think about you. As these situations don't necessarily require running or fighting, as they did in our ancestral times, the hormones remain within the body. Unless we do something physical to release them, there's a cumulative effect. By consciously walking, running, participating in sports, gardening or DIY, we can bring the body back into balance. Relaxation also helps by activating hormones that can calm your fight-or-flight symptoms. Meditation, breathing, yoga or anything else you find relaxing can help. It's about learning what works for you

How anxiety can be beneficial

As well as incorporating exercise and relaxation to manage the symptoms of anxiety, it's also important to address what's triggering it in the first place. Anxiety like all emotions has a useful purpose. Anxiety enables us to perform at our best in exams and other events. Anxiety alerts you to the importance of something and helps you prepare for it. If you didn't worry about whether you'll get it all done, you wouldn't organize yourself. Naturally, you'll feel anxious before an interview or a first date, which helps you realize it's something meaningful to you.

If you're going through change, it's natural to feel anxious and realising this highlights the need for more support to help you with the adjustment. If you're facing a difficult conversation or worrying about the outcome, you're likely to plan or practice what to do. In all of these scenarios, the anxiety prompts you to take steps so that you're prepared. It's trying to help you towards the best possible outcome. Anxiety also helps keep us safe. If you're walking alone and have an anxious feeling about a particular road, it's important to listen to that. If you listen to your vulnerability, you can take steps towards safety. Knowing you're anxious in the dark encourages you to travel with others.

In an ideal world, you'd be in tune with your body. You'd recognize the signs of anxiety and acknowledge the important message. You'd take appropriate action such as reading about the new situation or asking your friends for clothing advice before your date or interview. You'd also build in time for exercise or relaxation when your body needs it to help alleviate the fight-or-flight symptoms and accept anxiety as important information. Life can be much easier when we accept who we are and our feelings.

Dealing with overwhelming anxiety

What if you don't know why you're anxious though, or can't stop the spiralling thoughts? Sometimes, anxiety becomes overwhelming and constant. It can be hard to recognize the message as everything's a worry. You're constantly flooded with the fight-or-flight feeling and it seems impossible to relax. Naturally, you'll probably want to get rid of your anxiety. You hope that if you ignore it, it'll just go away. I completely understand why you'd want to do this. Anxiety like this can be excruciating. Unfortunately though, ignoring it doesn't work. The anxiety, even though it may seem unruly, is actually trying to help. Whether it's avoiding danger or preparing for something important, turning off anxiety would prevent this. Also, ignoring it brings layers of judgement and resistance, and we've already seen how that adds to the problem in Chapter 1 – it's effectively fighting fear with fear. Rather than helping it, the situation becomes worse. It's a bit like shouting at somebody who's shouting at you. It escalates and the message gets totally lost.

Imagine you've an assignment deadline. You weren't expecting it and you've got a really full week with rehearsals for an upcoming play. It's your mum's birthday, you haven't got a present yet and you've arranged to see your friends. The thought of the assignment is just too much. You're so overwhelmed that you just can't face thinking about it. You've had a niggling feeling all day about starting the research but there's been just too much other stuff in your head. You go to bed hoping you'll feel better in the morning. You can't sleep though. You keep thinking you need to start your research. You need a particular reference and go online but you can't find it. You worry about not finding it and this spirals into what if I can't do the assignment? Within five minutes, you've jumped to: 'I might lose my friends, my family will be upset with me, I'll be lonely forever...' Sleep now seems impossible. Sound familiar? Everyone's been here at some point.

What started out as an anxious thought is now a sick feeling in your stomach, preventing you from sleeping, and a constant feeling of dread. The original reason for the anxiety is lost amid a cycle of overwhelming anxious thoughts. You can't even see that it started with the assignment and that problem-solving how to get hold of the research could help. Instead, you feel overwhelmed with worry and find it hard to be objective or spot the flaws within the thinking. When anxiety feels so heightened, it's hard to make good decisions. By trying to minimize the anxious symptoms, you start to avoid situations. You might avoid further studying or a new job, going to a party or meeting new people. These things may be what you'd actually love to do deep down, but they're lost within the overwhelm.

What helps anxiety?

So what can be done? The first step is learning to recognize the signs that you're anxious. There are many ways to do this, such as Guided Meditation 10 – Body Awareness Scan (see Chapter 13) or remembering to notice, several times a day, any physical symptoms that might indicate fight or flight. Some people find that writing a list of their thoughts from the day can highlight whether they're anxious or stressed.

Even if you're unsure when you're anxious, building in time for regular relaxation and exercise can help prevent the cumulative build-up of the stress hormones. Having a repertoire of spontaneous options is helpful, such as a quick walk or run around the block or taking a break. Another helpful strategy is to use a breathing practice. Breathing helps slow you down and connect you to yourself. A few moments of deep breathing can help release hormones that reduce the stress response. When you're anxious, you shallow breathe. When you're relaxed, you breathe more deeply. Have you ever noticed a baby breathing? There is a clear rise and fall of the stomach. We come into the world knowing how to breathe but pick up bad habits along the way.

Exercise 9: Deep breath

You can use this breathing exercise whenever you need it and wherever you are. If you feel in any way self-conscious, you could pop off to the bathroom, or anywhere else private you can find. Practising this deep breathing technique a couple of times a day, when you're not feeling anxious, will bring the most benefits.

1. Take a really deep breath deep through your nose into your stomach, which expands your abdomen and diaphragm. You should really feel this in your stomach.
2. Hold your breath for a second or two as long as this feels comfortable.
3. Then, on the out breath, also through your nose, breathe very slowly out, releasing all of your tension and stress.

The out breath is important as this helps to release the stress hormones and tension so the longer and slower the better. If you're not noticing any movement in your stomach, you may be shallow breathing. It does take practice and you will notice the difference the more you practice. It's not uncommon to feel tired or other emotion after doing so as this is often masked by the stress hormones. Breathing helps you to be more in touch with your body. Regular exercise can also help you to breathe more deeply.

Exercise 10: Overcoming panic breath

If you are having a panic attack, it will be very difficult to breathe deeply (as in Exercise 9 above). It's hard to go from shallow breathing to deep breathing straightaway. So you might want to imagine yourself as a lift and gradually move from shallow breathing to deeper breathing, one floor at a time. It may take a few minutes to reach your abdomen and it doesn't matter if you don't reach it. Your goal is to very gently and gradually slow down your breathing.

Remember:

- The more that you practise deep breathing when you're not feeling anxious, the easier this process will be.
- Tell yourself you are OK and your symptoms are the result of your feeling of panic.
- Unless you are genuinely concerned for your safety, tell yourself that you are safe and that the feeling will pass.
- Distract yourself if necessary by thinking of something completely different.

I sometimes imagine anxious thoughts are like aeroplanes circling round around the airport trying to land. If you write the thoughts down, they can land on the page. It helps to prevent the repetition of the same thoughts over and over. The following exercise can help you do this, as well as helping you to understand the reason for your anxiety. By identifying this, you're acknowledging the message the anxiety is trying to convey and separating it from the spiralling unhelpful thoughts.

Exercise 11: Helping anxiety do its job

When you're feeling anxious it can be helpful to write down your thoughts by using the following example as a template.

Anxious thoughts	What's helpful? What action might help to improve the scenario or reduce the worry? (Usually thoughts closest to the present tense.)	What thoughts can challenge the spiralling anxious thoughts (usually more future-orientated and assumption-based thoughts)? Consider the evidence that it's not true, as well as alternative viewpoints and handling the worst-case scenario. What's a more empowering thought?
Example 1: 'I might not pass this exam.'	Tell yourself the anxiety you are experiencing is helping you to improve your chances of passing. What steps can you take to help? Who might be able to help you? For example, you could create an action plan that helps you realize you have enough time. If you do, keep telling yourself you have enough time to do well. If time is short, what plans can you make for the best?	Challenge any unhelpful thoughts by acknowledging that you're working on a plan and doing the best that you can. If there's any justice, you will succeed (see also Chapter 11 for more on using affirmations). Write down all of the exams and assignments you've passed to date. If you've worked hard, why should this be any different? Even if you were to fail, what's the worst-case scenario? For example, retake the exam, learn from what you didn't do well in, find a different path, etc. Remind yourself that failure makes us stronger.

Continued

How confident are you about your strategy to do well? Do you need to improve your revision skills, change your study environment, revise with others, practise with past exam papers, learn from previous exams that have gone well, manage distractions, reduce stress, take a break, get support from a tutor or someone else?	If you've failed in the past, what did you learn from it and what did you act on? If you're doing something differently and working hard, tell yourself you're doing the best that you can.
	It's unlikely parents or friends will stop caring for you. The person who is likely to be the most disappointed is yourself.
Even if you really have left your revision to the last minute and there's a genuine chance of failing, you still need to act. Talk to somebody and consider your options. Even if you do receive some harsh words (justified or not), you'll be able to stop worrying as you'll understand what's next.	
Consider what you could do differently next time to avoid being in the same situation. Tell yourself you're human, everybody makes mistakes and learn from this one.	

Continued

Example 2: 'I'm nervous about meeting new people.'	What might help you to feel better about the situation? For example, going with someone else, arranging to meet somebody that you know or confiding in a friend and asking them to help you meet new people.	Acknowledge it's natural to be nervous when you meet new people and the symptoms you are experiencing are understandable. Remind yourself of all the things you're doing to help you feel better about the situation from the middle column.
	Watching and learning from people who you think are good at this. Notice their strategies and try to find a way to utilise them in a way that's comfortable for you.	Note how many times in your life you've met somebody new and everything was fine. (Every friend you met for the first time at some point)
	Think about some topics that might be helpful to discuss or have some questions to ask other people. People like to be asked about themselves.	Consider all the reasons why you're likeable. The worst situation is likely to be that you have no one to talk to. Identify some people you could go up to, and consider going to the bathroom or for a walk in this time. Remind yourself that other people probably won't notice and that your nervousness will be fairly well hidden. Everyone has moments like this.
	Tell yourself the anxiety you're experiencing is identifying an opportunity for you to feel more confident in yourself. Take steps to build your confidence and self-esteem (see Chapter 7), and identify books, courses or other ways.	Remind yourself that no one can be friends with everyone and that even if you don't meet anyone new, you have lots of friends already.

Hopefully, the above exercise will help you to understand your anxiety and the steps that would be helpful to address the situation. It also highlights how the spiralling thoughts aren't necessarily true. Sometimes when we're in something, it's hard to spot a way forwards. You might benefit from seeking support from someone who you trust to help you, such as a teacher, parent, friend or other professional. Going through the worst possible scenario can be helpful if you're prepared to consider this. You might have uncomfortable feelings at first but hopefully, you'll be able to see that it's not as bad as you think and you'll cope. Many people fear they'll let their parents down or their friendships will suffer, but once they say it out loud, they realize it's probably not true. Talking with your parents or friends about their expectations and dealing with challenges might prevent anxiety in the first place.

It's worth noting we judge ourselves more harshly than anybody else would. We base our assumptions about how other people will act based on our own judgements. So if you think no one would like you if you failed, it's probably because you wouldn't like the fact you've failed. Identifying stories and triggers to your anxiety can be helpful. Working on themes, such as fear of judgement, fear of getting it wrong, fear of being unwell and fear of failure, can prevent their occurrence. You can do this by revisiting Chapter 3 or trying Exercise 12 below.

Understanding the anxious part

We all get anxious, although the degree and frequency varies from person to person; it's another continuum if it helps you to see it in this way. There's a theory of subpersonalities from Psychosynthesis counselling which offers a useful perspective in understanding your anxiety. Diana Whitmore describes subpersonalities as psychological identities that coexist within one person.[1] You can probably relate to the idea of having different parts – perhaps an anxious part, a critical part, a hard-working part, a part that wants to lounge around all day, and so on. We probably all have a different list although there may be some similarities. The quality and dominance of these parts will vary though as each subpersonality is formed in response to our unique experiences.

Each subpersonality has its own behaviour and needs and is likely to have been developed subconsciously to help you in some way. For example, if you experienced something painful or upsetting when you were growing up, you possibly developed an anxious part to protect you from experiencing the same again. It doesn't have to be one main event and could be several smaller situations. As this was a subconscious process, you're unlikely to have evaluated the effectiveness. By understanding your subpersonalities, you're able to see them from a bigger perspective.

Exercise 12: Understanding the anxious part of you[2]

This exercise can help you be more conscious of your anxious part and adapt it to be more effective. Identifying that anxiety is a part of you rather than your complete identity can also help it to feel more manageable.

Close your eyes and get a sense of your anxious part. Imagine it in front of you. This may come immediately or you might find it helpful to remember recent scenarios. Trust the first thing that comes into your head as you write down the answers to the following:

• If this part of you was a character/colour/symbol/shape or had a name what would it be? (See what image comes to you or you might resonate more with a feeling or sound. You can just call it your anxious part if you prefer. Describe anything about your anxious part. The quality of it. The intensity of it.)

- What are the disadvantages of having this part?
- How is it trying to help you? How does it try to protect you?
- How could you modify this anxious part of you so that it could do the job it's trying to help you with, without the disadvantages?

With the image, it might be a pointy shape, a black cloud or you could just call it the anxious part. The disadvantages could be physical symptoms, holding yourself back, self-criticism, constant worry, sadness, difficulty experiencing happiness, et cetera.

If it's hard for you to see how your anxious part is trying to help, recall a time when you felt anxious. It might help to call upon a time when you were younger, as this will help you to understand it more. For example, you may have moved to a new house and changed schools. This was a really tough experience for you. You probably found it difficult to meet new friends. The new school friends weren't necessarily unkind – they were just playing their usual games with their established friends. You missed your old friends. You missed the games you were used to and the conversations that felt familiar. You were grieving for this loss which was upsetting and painful to experience. You didn't feel confident or happy. It's hard when you feel like this to meet new friends. Even if you did make friends quickly, it was a while before you felt included. You felt lonely and sad and feared the situation wouldn't improve.

Even when the situation did improve and you felt happy with some new friends, the anxiety remained. The feelings of sadness and loneliness were so uncomfortable at the time, you created an anxious part of you to defend against experiencing them again. As a result, you started to feel anxious in any new situation. Subconsciously you believed if you worried about possible situations, you could prevent them from happening. You could avoid future uncomfortable feelings. So the anxious part was created to help you avoid experiencing difficult feelings ever again. It was created for a positive reason although, as it was subconscious, it wasn't necessarily designed in the most effective way.

Now you can see this, you can evaluate its success. You can see it's impossible for it to succeed. You can never stop the ups and downs of life. Not only that, you can see that it's still trying to do the same job today even though it's maybe 5, 10, or even more years later. Instead of stopping uncomfortable situations from happening, you feel anxious frequently. This may actually be worse than the occasional difficult feeling. It also doesn't stop the inevitable pain from life's ups and downs. You end up feeling it anyway. On top of that, the anxiety also prevents you from going to things you may actually enjoy. Before now, you assumed the sick feeling was a physical illness. Now, you realize your upset tummy is a natural human reaction when you're facing a situation that triggers the fight-or-flight response.

By making this all conscious, you can help the situation by modifying how the subpersonality works for you. Each time you feel anxious, you can acknowledge it's not a pest to get rid of but a friend trying to help. You can acknowledge the butterflies as a normal reaction. You can be objective about your reservations as you can see they're not necessarily your truth. There's a difference between an intuitive feeling not to do something and fear to try new things. You're reframing that the anxiety is trying to help you be happy. Each time you feel it you can acknowledge, 'I'm feeling anxious as I want this to go well but staying home isn't going to help me do that.'

You can also start considering the benefits of going out and what steps could help you feel more positive about the situation? For example, seeking support from people that you trust, asking friends to go with you, telling yourself that the anxiety is trying to help you rather than stopping you. Tell yourself that life has ups and downs. Make a list of all of the times you were worried about something and it was actually better than you thought. Before you changed schools, how many positive situations did you experience? Are you OK now? You might like to imagine your image of your anxious part as a slightly different colour or shape which helps some people to work with it more effectively.

Hopefully, you now have a better understanding of anxiety and your own triggers. Additional chapters that can help specifically are chapter 7 on self-esteem and Chapter 13 on embracing peace.

When to seek professional help

If your anxiety is as a result of experiencing or witnessing something traumatic, e.g. an accident, or if you're experiencing nightmares or flashbacks alongside your feelings of anxiety, it's advisable to seek professional support from a doctor or counsellor. Always seek professional help if your symptoms are affecting you severely over a longer period of time or if you're at risk of harm in any way.

Summary

- When you're stressed or facing something important or that you fear you may not cope with, your body triggers a fight-or-flight response. Doing something physical or relaxing enables the body to come back to balance and helps dispel the symptoms.
- Anxiety is essentially trying to help you. Exploring any triggers for anxiety can help you to act to improve your safety or chances of success.
- When anxiety becomes problematic, challenging distorted thinking and understanding the anxious part can help you to manage it more effectively. Ignoring anxiety or banishing it is a counter-productive strategy.

Chapter 7

BUILDING
SELF-ESTEEM

Along with anxiety and depression, self-esteem is one of the commonest reasons for people seeking counselling where I work.[1] We all experience difficult life events and change, and these naturally affect our confidence and how we see ourselves. Self-esteem affects all ages as life events and changes are constant. As there is so much change when we are younger, the impact can be felt a lot more. As with other situations not typically spoken about, it's easy to assume you're the only one facing self-esteem issues, which only serves to add additional layers of difficulty through judgements and resistance. By remembering we're all human, facing ups and downs, this can help prevent these additional layers from forming.

In Chapter 3 we explored our inner dialogue, our story. Thoughts such as, 'I'm not good enough, attractive enough, funny enough or I'm rubbish at this or that.' These beliefs are formed during these difficult life events as we try to make sense of them. We project these beliefs onto other people and imagine this is what they think of us. The reality reflects our own perception. Our own low self-esteem. Instead of worrying about the perception of others and trying to change that, it would be more effective to work on building your own confidence and self-esteem, and create an internal focus rather than an external one.

Self-esteem as a continuum

Rather than having either low or high self-esteem, I like to imagine it as more of a continuum. We all go up and down the continuum frequently depending on the day we've had or what's happening in our life. During times of change, it's usual to have a dip in self-esteem. Events that can cause a dip include relationship difficulties of any kind, including friends, family, teachers and more intimate relationships. Divorce, bereavement, moving home, school, starting university or a new job. Even everyday events, such as giving presentations, competing in a sports event, showing your artwork and meeting new people, can have an impact. People who've experienced bullying or who feel criticized by others will naturally feel less confident. If you feel pressure from others, you'll feel you have something to prove and maybe not feel good enough.

It's not going through these things per se that causes low self-esteem but how you interpret the event and the subsequent stories that arise (see also Chapter 3). If you relate to the difficulty as being partly your fault rather than an everyday life event, it can be more pronounced and last longer. By working on your self-esteem, you can take positive steps along the continuum. The more work, the greater the rewards. If you accept it's natural to have a dip in confidence while facing difficult events, it's easier to cope with. It doesn't mean you relish them but hopefully, you can stop dreading them.

What is low self-esteem?

What do we actually mean by low self-esteem? You can spot whether you have a tendency for low self-esteem if you recognize several of the following signs:

- You dislike yourself – perhaps your body image or personality.
- You put yourself down.
- You believe others are better than you.
- You have higher standards for yourself than you do for other people.
- You focus more on your negative points than your strengths.
- You're pessimistic about the future.
- You let other people make decisions for you.
- You're self-loathing or self-critical.
- You'd rather please others than yourself.
- You hold yourself back from positive situations, e.g. activities, job interviews and social situations.
- You cringe at praise.
- You avoid conflict.
- You find it hard to stand up for yourself.

Everyone's likely to recognize themselves in this list but it's about how often and how this affects you. After a bad day or during a difficult period, you'll naturally recognize more of these factors. If you frequently feel low as a result of your self-esteem, form less healthy relationships and use unhelpful coping strategies, you'd benefit from working on your self-esteem. Self-destructive behaviours, such as using food, alcohol or drugs to escape the accompanying difficult feelings, further reinforce the cycle of low self-esteem.

On the contrary, someone with higher self-esteem is more often likely to feel confident and happy in themselves. As a result, they make decisions comfortably without giving power away to others. They typically see themselves in a more positive light and have the resilience to cope with setbacks. It's not that difficult things don't affect them, it's that they see them more as one of those things, rather than a personal failing. It's easier to bounce back as a result. People with higher self-esteem typically build healthier relationships with love and respect. They can hear praise and constructive criticism. They recognize they've got strengths and talents as well as areas that require more work. It's part of being human. It's also easier for them to be assertive.

Exercise 13: Understanding your self-esteem

Assess your level of self-esteem and where this might come from by answering the following questions:

- Where on the continuum of self-esteem would you put yourself? (On a scale of 1-10 where 1 = very low self-esteem, 10 = very high self-esteem.)
- Identify times in your life where you've had higher self-esteem? What beliefs did you hold about yourself and situations?
- Write down the areas of self-esteem that could be worked on. You might list some of the points from the list above. For example, pleasing others, avoiding conflict. You might connect this to the stories you identified in Chapter 3.
- Reflect on possible life events that have contributed to these stories and your low self-esteem.

Now you have some more understanding of your self-esteem, let's look at what can help increase it.

Only one perspective

Your perspective of your self-esteem is not necessarily the truth. It's just your opinion and it's not necessarily the same opinion as others. Remember you see yourself through a unique pair of glasses. Your story. You might not like yourself but your friends and family could think you're one of the nicest people in the world. As they think this, they imagine you already know and so don't tell you. Even if they did, we know from Chapter 3 that you're likely to reject evidence which doesn't match your own belief. Self-esteem isn't a fact, it's not fixed and it can be changed. The more you work on understanding the full picture, the more you can build your self-esteem. Let's now consider other possible perspectives in order to do so.

Exercise 14: Identify alternative interpretations

Consider each of the life events which you wrote down in the exercise above and identify alternative interpretations of the story. You don't have to believe them but just acknowledge that there are different ways to view the situation. If you find this difficult, try putting yourself in somebody else's shoes. You might find it helpful to reflect on the questions just before Exercise 6, Challenging your story (in chapter 3), to help you challenge your thoughts.

For example, you might connect your low self-esteem to an experience of bullying. Your interpretation was that you weren't good enough or not likeable enough. On reflection, you can see other possibilities. The bully targeted several people – it wasn't just you. It might say more about the bully than you. What was going on for the bully? Were they having difficulties in other aspects of their life? Were they insecure? Rather than being not good enough or likeable enough, was it a reflection that you were in the wrong place at the wrong time? Did they pick on you as you hadn't yet learned to stand up for yourself? Did the opportunity encourage you to be more assertive or find a different group of friends? The bully, if they were within your friendship group, wasn't a compatible friend. Were they jealous of you in some way?

If your date didn't call when they said they would, you're probably imagining you said something wrong or they don't fancy you. You're probably feeling low, frustrated with yourself and possibly shame. We've all been there at some point – even the people we think are really attractive and immune from rejection. I've had the benefit of working with a lot of people and know for a fact that we all experience rejection. We all have crises of confidence from time to time and it's tough to feel this.

It can help to pause and consider other possible interpretations. Take time out before you convince yourself it's the truth and life will never be the same again. Maybe there's a good reason why they didn't call. There might be something going on for them or they had a shocker of a day. They may have lost your number. Maybe they think you're not interested in them. Maybe they like you too much and that feels too scary to start a relationship. Even if it doesn't work out, it doesn't mean you're unlikable or unlovable, just that it didn't work out with this person. Maybe there's somebody out there more compatible for you. Or it's not the right time for one or both of you.

Spending too much time agonizing over what you think is going on causes upset and angst. It's loaded with assumptions and inevitably causes a cycle of negative thinking and often much pain. Exploring alternatives and reminding yourself that it's not necessarily the truth will hopefully help to calm this down. It's more effective to do something you enjoy, talk to people who care about you and deal with the actual situation when it arises. Seeking feedback from people you trust can be helpful as it helps to see other possibilities. Sometimes when you're 'in something', it can feel huge and overwhelming and you may need to nurture yourself with extra self-care. Choose another day to step back from this and you might see a broader perspective.

The more you can identify there are different possibilities and interpretations, the more you can cast doubt on whether the belief is solid and the only truth. Each time you face a new situation that triggers the painful emotion of your original story, try to consider other perspectives. Over time, you'll be able to choose which version of events or story you wish to believe. A further helpful way of doing this is included in Chapter 11. Remember one event in the present is not a prediction of every event in the future. Everyone faces rejection and difficulty at some point – it's part of being human. The pain you experience at the time is not everlasting and we grow and learn from tough situations.

Develop a nurturing critic

To help you challenge your perspective, it helps to modify your inner voice. As we explored in the previous chapter, viewing yourself made up of different parts or subpersonalities can help you to do this. Everyone can probably relate to an inner critic. This is the part that says you could try harder. You're not doing it right. You look stupid. Everyone else is better than you. While everybody has an inner critic, the degree of criticism varies from mildly critical to downright rude. Where would you put yours?

This critical part was probably created when you were much younger. Potentially in your early school years when someone made you feel stupid. Or you were told off by a teacher or your parents and felt belittled. It doesn't matter how big or small the scenario was, just how you reacted to it. If you felt ashamed, you probably wanted to avoid it ever happening again. Remember the shame shields in Chapter 4. The critic may have been subconsciously created to prevent you ever being told off again and tries to tell you off first to avoid this. The critic is probably trying to help you to be liked, prevent you from further hurt, achieve your best or something similar. This is a good intention but rather distorted, as how can you always get it right if you don't know what the other person wants or how to deliver this? Even if you could, is the constant internal criticism better than a telling off that may not even happen?

Exercise 15: Understanding the critic[2]

Now we've highlighted the possible intention of the critic, let's look at modifying it to be more effective.

- If the critical voice was a character/colour/shape or had a name, what would it be? (It might help to close your eyes and just get in touch with the critical voice and see what image comes to you. Or you can do this as a written exercise.)
- What are the disadvantages of having this critical voice?
- How is it trying to help you? Consider the examples above.
- How could you modify your critic so it's more effective? E.g. change the colour or model it on someone motivational and nurturing.

After doing this exercise, I often ask clients to think of the best and worst teacher they can remember. Most people can remember a critical teacher who used humiliation and putdowns to motivate by fear. Some say this made them want to prove the teacher wrong but most found this strategy altogether unhelpful or ineffective in the long term. Conversely, they describe a teacher who was supportive, encouraging and kind who got the best results out of them. This teacher challenged and pushed them in a motivational way. People are often surprised to realize that their critic is more similar to the critical teacher who got the worst results out of them. Identifying this alongside the positive intention of the critic enables them to model their critic on a more positive and motivational role model. It doesn't have to be a teacher, it could be anyone in your life that motivated and supported you.

To help the critic get the best out of you, try to catch yourself mid-criticism. Acknowledge it's trying to help you. Trying to ignore it won't work but acknowledging and thanking it will. Try to find a kinder and more motivational way to say the same thing. Instead of thinking 'You're rubbish at your job,' acknowledge you're not feeling good about your job. The criticism is trying to help you improve. What's the reality? It might be you're doing better than you think. In which case, you can tell yourself that things are going well and you're trying your best. Taking steps to improve your confidence and self-esteem could help you.

If there's an issue in reality, what action would be helpful? Actually working on the issue and telling yourself that you're trying hard to address it is better than constant criticism and no action. Talking to your employer or a colleague might help you progress. Or it might be that there's another job more suitable for you. Either way acknowledging that the self-criticism is actually trying to help you improve your performance, your confidence or help you progress on a different path is more effective than repetitive self-criticism. Telling yourself off doesn't help the situation but doing something about it does. It also helps alleviate the resulting low mood.

Negative comments aren't necessarily the truth

In the same way that your perspective of the world is just your view, it's the same for somebody else. If somebody says you're irritating or selfish, it doesn't necessarily mean that you are. They may be reacting in the moment or triggered by their own stories. There may be a misunderstanding. Even if there's a grain of truth in it, they're talking about your behaviour, not you as a person. One or even several selfish or irritating acts doesn't mean you are selfish or irritating.

We're all kind, funny, hard-working, irritating, selfish, and so on from time to time. We need to discern how much we take on other people's comments. You could work on the trait if you believe there's some truth in it.

Remember we're all human with opportunities to grow. We all make mistakes and we learn from them. People who love and care about you will accept your limitations and support you even if you're selfish or irritating at times. Try to bear this in mind when you're receiving any criticism. Knowing how criticism affects you, can you help another by initiating a positive cycle? It might also help you to notice and receive more positive feedback from others.

Exercise 16: Initiate a positive cycle of feedback

Practice telling others what you value in them and the important qualities that you have noticed. It's highly likely that if your self-esteem needs a boost, then others would benefit from a boost too.

Tell your family members and friends what you're grateful for, what you appreciate them doing for you, and what you value in them as a person.

You'll feel good through this act of giving, probably start to notice more positive things in yourself and be more open to receiving compliments from others, which will hopefully generate a positive cycle.

Self-acceptance

Now we understand more about self-esteem, where it comes from in our own lives and have started to challenge its foundations, let's turn our attention to building self-esteem. We're all different. We come in various shapes and sizes and that's a biological fact. We all have different personalities, strengths, hobbies and interests. We have different beliefs, religions, race, sexuality, dress sense, abilities. We're diverse. We're all unique. We're wonderfully human. This means we're not all attracted to or get on with the same people. We're compatible with certain people and not others. As we have different talents, we naturally do well at some things and less well at others. This is wonderful and also very practical as there are lots of friends, partners, jobs and hobbies to go round. It's impossible to be all things to all people.

Yet we devote so much time wishing and striving to be a different person. We have sometimes punishing expectations about what we *should* look like. We can berate ourselves for one friendship or intimate relationship not working out. We can feel sad if we're not as good at football as somebody else. I understand the longing for wanting to fit in. We want to be the same as others. The grass is greener. We're human.

These influences are deep-seated and come from our experiences, stories, cultural expectations, media pressures, etc. I went to a training day recently on body dysmorphia run by a colleague. We saw how technology can alter people's photographs on the screen. I was horrified how ordinary blemishes, natural curves and shapes were easily changed into some unrealistic image. We're bombarded by beautiful images. Flawless skin. Slim figures. We don't give any thought to how real it is. Many celebrities are now banning airbrushing as it perpetuates beauty myths that are simply not true. If only we could do the same on social media on the perception of perfect lives.

You can learn new skills and modify your appearance but you can't fundamentally change who you are or what you look like. Even if you could, it reinforces the ladder concept from Chapter 1, Going with the Flow of Life: 'I'll be happy when I've changed…' Think about how much energy is wasted on a cause which is virtually impossible to attain. However, imagine what would happen if that energy was directed towards loving and accepting who you are and what you do have. This is a challenge with much greater odds of success and rewards at the end of it. Finding the people who do genuinely like you and are naturally attracted to you will be a much happier challenge.

A healthier approach for a happier result

A healthier approach is to embrace who you already are. If you like and accept yourself, you're more likely to take better care of yourself, such as having an exercise regime, taking care of your appearance, and giving yourself good food and sleep. I'm not saying that changing your perspective towards acceptance is going to bring instantaneous happiness. Building self-esteem is a journey but at least you're on the right road rather than going down a dead-end.

If you believe in yourself and have self-love and acceptance, you'll become more attractive to others. Look at people around you who are confident and happy in themselves. They seem to radiate this and it's magnetic to others. Remember how powerful our beliefs can be. You start to attract others who can accept and appreciate this in you. Conversely, someone who's attractive but not happy in themselves, might attract more attention initially but not necessarily successful relationships. I've been running self-esteem groups for nearly eight years and when the discussion of what's attractive comes up, there's unanimous agreement that its personality and a positive vibe that's most attractive. The good news is that we can all work on our personality and attitude to life.

Exercise 17: Body gratitude

Write down everything that you are grateful for with your body. For example, 'I love my hair/my skin, etc. Or, 'I like…' if love is too strong a word. If this is a real challenge, try looking at it from one or more of the following perspectives:

- My eyes allow me to see beautiful things in the world, my lungs enable me to breathe fresh air, I can run, I can laugh, I can sing, I can dance.
- My body has healed [insert condition].'
- My body gives me signals about when to rest, being able to swim in the sea, savouring the taste of food, feeling the elements on my skin, being able to hug and have physical closeness with another.

A simple way to increase your self-esteem can be to avoid using social media too often because it doesn't give an accurate reflection of reality. Never take a measure of your self-esteem from this. There can be some very cruel and unhelpful comments, and not necessarily from anyone that you would ordinarily ask an opinion from. At the body dysmorphia training day, I was hugely affected by a growing trend of teenagers posting images of themselves and asking strangers if they were attractive. The individual sometimes received hundreds of comments. Some were lovely kind responses but there were also some mean and potentially damaging ones. It took me several days to shake off the sad feeling. I was disturbed by how cruel people could be to someone so vulnerable. It further ignited my passion to work on this book. Learn to listen to yourself and the people who care about you. Measure yourself by your actions, behaviours, intentions rather than the number of likes that you receive. Use social media for fun and for positive means only.

Internal measures of self-esteem

As we've seen, focusing on being liked, not being rejected, being the best at sports and all other external measures of self-esteem sets you up for disappointment. By external, I mean reliant on other people's opinions or factors outside of our control. It's hard to measure being liked as we don't know what other people are thinking. We can't measure rejection as we don't know how everyone would react in the world. A much more reliable and helpful way is to measure ourselves from an internal focus. How we believe we've done rather than relying on praise from others, your effort and progress rather than the achievement of a mark, your intention rather than the outcome. Try it for yourself in the following exercise:

Exercise 18: Looking for positives

Write down five things you're proud of every day. It can be from the day or something you remember from the past. It might be an achievement, something new you've learned or tried, something that helped somebody else or when you've tried your best. Examples could include completing a project that you were procrastinating about, helping out around the house, supporting a friend, improving on a skill or hobby even if you haven't yet quite achieved what you'd like, learning to cook something new, being able to accept a positive comment, being kind to yourself, getting involved in a cause, complementing somebody else and so on.

While learning a new skill, attaining a good grade or being picked for a team is something positive, just looking for these things relies on external validation rather than rewarding you for who you are.

Add any compliments, any positive qualities or strengths you recognize in yourself.

We have no idea what impact we have on others so please write down anything that you can think of, even if it feels small – e.g. planting some flowers in the garden which might brighten up many people who pass by, smiling at somebody in the street who you don't know. These are, in effect, examples of sending love and positive thoughts to somebody whether they know it or not.

This exercise may be difficult at first as you are so used to looking for the negative with self-esteem. However the more you do it, the more it will help you to build self-esteem. If you're finding this really hard, you can either think about it from the perspective of your best friend, parent or someone that you trust or ask them directly. Do this for at least 21 days or for as long as it feels good.

Learn to trust you

You're the best person to have an opinion about you. You know your thoughts, your intent. You know what's best for you and what makes you happy. I appreciate sometimes it's hard to know these things. It takes practice and trust but the more you do it, the easier it gets. Try to determine your own choices and opinions rather than allowing others to answer for you. Respect who you are, learn to love and look after yourself and make the choices that will bring you the most joy. You can improve your awareness of yourself through all of the exercises and guided meditations in this book and by focusing on yourself as the best source of information. Of course, other people can help you by acting as a sounding board, offering perspectives that help you to see the bigger picture and offering suggestions but it's important that it's your truth. Here's an exercise that can help.

Exercise 19: Making decisions

Identify a decision that you need to make. It can be something as simple as what drink you would like, which social outing to choose or which job to take. Identify the different options and ideally narrow down your decision to two or three of them. This exercise is harder to follow with too many available choices. Now use the following process to help you reach a decision:

1. Ground yourself by imagining you are a tree with roots going into the ground. Imagine branches going out through your head and connecting to the sun. Visualize a golden bubble of protection around you and take some deep breaths.
2. Close your eyes and imagine each possible scenario in turn. If it's a choice between a glass of water or an orange juice, bring up the image of each one separately. Imagine drinking each one or picture yourself after finishing the drink.
3. For each scenario, notice any colours, shapes, sounds, and what sensations you have in your body. You might have a symbol, a quality or you might sense how bright and clear the image or feeling is. You might like to draw and reflect on them afterwards.
4. How do you make sense of the different experiences? Hopefully, the different experiences bring clarity of what you intuitively prefer. If there's not much in it, it might be the options are equally beneficial. The more you practice, the easier this exercise becomes.
5. Alternatively, you might prefer to write a list of pros and cons for each option. You'll probably notice that you start to add additional notes in the column which represent the choice you want deep down.

Remember that if you make the wrong decision, it will simply give you information to help you make more informed choices in the future. In most situations, you can correct something if you discover it was wrong and if you can't, stay trusting that something positive you haven't seen yet is around the corner.

Self-esteem as a form of protection

Sometimes it can be hard to build self-esteem and it feels as though there's a block to moving forwards. Many people find it difficult to get past the idea of their story not being true. Imagine feeling unattractive to others and having experienced rejection many times. You probably can't hear that your story isn't necessarily the truth. You can't see that attractiveness is a subjective thing and your belief may be self-fulfilling (see also Chapter 3). You're probably hurting and feel demoralised. My heart goes out to you. This is painful to acknowledge but I hope it helps you to know this is a common situation. It's not down to you being unable to change. It's not because your self-esteem is necessarily the truth. It's probably due to you not being quite ready to move on. Let me explain.

Believing you're unattractive probably feels safer to you right now – it's part of your protection. If you continue believing this, you're unlikely to test out the theory. In doing so, you reduce the likelihood of any more painful rejection. On the other hand, if you entertain the idea that your story isn't the truth, you may have to test it out. Taking a risk can feel scary. There's a possibility of rejection. No wonder you may want to ignore me right now. Can I suggest reading on with the goal of understanding yourself? You don't have to do anything different unless you choose to.

Challenging your belief isn't about opening yourself up to more pain. It's never wise to take away your protection. If we understand more about our beliefs and how effective they are in protecting us, we might find that modification is more effective. Keeping yourself away from everybody to avoid rejection prevents further pain, but it also excludes the chance of experiencing positive emotions. You not only avoid rejection but also the chance of a relationship and happiness. Let's work with this block.

Exercise 20: Working with the block[3]
This exercise can help you bring awareness to any block you might be experiencing.

1. As in Exercise 19, start by grounding yourself by imagining you are a tree with roots going into the ground. Imagine branches going out through your head and connecting to the sun. Visualize a golden bubble of protection around you and take some deep breaths. Now use the following process:
2. Try to get a sense of what is holding you back from having good self-esteem. See sense and feel an image of your block. You might have a symbol, colour, feeling, sound. How big is this?
3. Draw or write down your experience.
4. How does the image protect you?
5. What impact does this have on you, your life and your self-esteem?
6. Are there any modifications you could make to your image that would help you move forwards but at the same time feel protected?

If you had an image of a wall, you might recognize that it keeps you at a distance from others. It helps you to avoid painful situations and keep you safe. You can also see that nothing positive gets through which affects your happiness. You also feel stuck and fear always being in this place. You'd like to put a window into the wall which you could open if you choose to. You can then feel the protection of the wall but also allow certain people, situations or positive emotions to enter. Consider how you could do this practically in your life. For example, do you meet all new people with the protection of the wall but, after a period of time, allow some people in who you trust? Maybe start by having the window open on occasions.

If you manage to understand your block and are open to modification, you might like to go back through the exercises in this chapter and throughout the book (see Appendix II for a list of them). If you didn't resonate with this exercise or didn't feel ready, you could try again another time or seek professional support. Remember that self-esteem is a journey. The more work you put into it, the more rewards available. Also, respect the times when you don't feel like working on yourself. Try to do it regularly and especially after experiencing any difficulty in life. Many of the chapters in Part III continue with further ideas.

> **When to seek professional help**
> Always seek professional help if your symptoms are affecting you severely over a longer period of time or if you're at risk of harm in any way.

Guided Meditation 5: The Seed

In this guided meditation you visualize yourself in full bloom and identify support to make this reality.

natalieread.online/seed

Summary

- Self-esteem is a continuum that you, and everyone else, constantly moves up and down depending on what's happening at the time, whether it's life events or life stages. The more work that you do on yourself, the more you can stay at the higher end of the continuum or avoid the extent of the dips.
- Your self-esteem reflects how you see yourself based on your perception and your assumptions. It's not a fact and not necessarily how other people see you.
- Acceptance of who you are is a much better use of your energy than battling to change who you fundamentally are.

There is a relationship between how much you love yourself and how much love you attract from others. It doesn't mean people don't love you when you don't love yourself but you're less likely to be able to see it and receive their love.

○ Reframing your inner critical voice, putting negative comments from others into perspective, initiating positive cycles of feedback, collating internal measures of self-esteem and limiting reliance on social media can all benefit your self-esteem.

○ Be aware of any blocks and protection because understanding and modifying them can help to improve their effectiveness, as it allows you to protect yourself without preventing you from experiencing the potential of happiness too.

Chapter 8

MANAGING ANGER

I don't have any anger. I'm not an angry person. I can't stop snapping at people for seemingly little things. I'm full of rage. My anger's getting out of control. I'm not usually angry but seem to be short with people. Whichever description best fits you, this chapter is equally for you. Anger affects everyone whether they acknowledge it or not. In Chapter 2, we saw how we form beliefs about emotions from our experiences. We learn how to 'do' anger from our experiences. As it's often subconscious, we have little control over it. This chapter helps in bringing awareness to your anger. The more you understand, acknowledge and work with your anger, the healthier it can be. Through awareness, we have more control.

There seems to be shame in our society about being angry. All human beings have all emotions and it's natural to experience anger from time to time. Like other emotions, anger has a purpose; it can be a reaction to feeling powerless, inadequate, misunderstood, victimized, embarrassed or in response to injustice, inequality, cruelty or brutality. If we didn't have anger, we wouldn't recognize this. We wouldn't feel passionate or have the energy to do something about it. Many good things have happened as a result of anger. Examples include the abolishment of the slave trade, the vote for women, peace agreements, campaigns for animal welfare and environmental protections. Despite this, anger is misunderstood and, as a result, can be denied.

Why is there a tendency to deny anger?

Past experiences of anger affect how you see it. You may have witnessed anger misused through aggression or violence. Anger may have been hidden or repressed because of ideas such as, 'We don't show anger in this family.' This may have been to the point you don't even realize you have anger. Instead, it may appear as passive aggression, occasional outbursts or through tears. We'll look at this more in a moment. Hollywood ideals and social media can also portray the idea of everyone being happy. Some movies show conflicts being worked through easily with a simple smile. This may give the impression that expressing anger in any other way is not the norm and can create shame –which further represses any feelings of anger. At the other end of the spectrum, movies can show frightening images of violence. Anger is then seen as something to be afraid of.

As a result, you may have received confusing messages about anger. You may subconsciously believe anger isn't safe, unacceptable or something to be avoided altogether. If so, you may try to deny any sense of it and repress it within. This can be so effective you actually imagine you don't have any anger. When it does surface, it can feel scary and overwhelming. Remember the pan analogy in Chapter 2. The lid holding the repressed emotion cannot hold it indefinitely. The result is an outburst of anger or it may simmer out as passive-aggressive. These experiences probably feel unsafe, further reinforcing the message anger is something to fear. The more you try to control anger by denying it, the more it becomes volatile and unpredictable.

Anger can be difficult to recognize

It can be confusing if you have a build-up of unexpressed anger from the past. For example, you experience something seemingly small, such as tripping over and hurting your toe. You feel stupid for not seeing the obstacle in your way. Your shame then turns to rage at the person who left the obstacle in such a silly place or the people you imagine are laughing at you. You can't see that they're not laughing at you in a mean way – this is your projection. You're feeling unkind towards yourself. You also feel stupid for tripping up in the first place. Why did you have to do that in front of everybody? You feel ashamed and embarrassed. The shame triggers your repressed anger inside. Before you know it, you're ranting at everyone in sight. When you do realize what's happening, you feel embarrassed by your outburst. You can see shock and horror on people's faces. You judge yourself for your reaction believing yourself to be a bad person. This reinforces your experience of shame. You feel even more angry, confused and upset by the whole scenario.

Anger can also be masked by other emotions. If you grew up believing that anger wasn't safe, you might show your anger through tears instead (so it looks like a different emotion). You may direct it towards yourself, as it might not feel safe to express your anger towards others. This is likely to lead to self-loathing and low self-esteem or even addictions and self-harm. You might have repressed your anger to such an extent that it manifests as depression – feeling numb and a lack of energy (see also Chapter 5). Repression of anger can also bring about anxiety, difficulty sleeping and physical ailments. All of these situations can make it harder to recognize the presence of anger and further perpetuate the myth that you don't have anger.

It can also work the other way where you feel so overwhelmed by anger that you don't believe you have other emotions. Frequently, anger masks emotions such as fear, insecurity, sadness, guilt and shame. For some people, these feelings may be more unpleasant and uncomfortable to feel than anger. We're all different. In this case, anger deflects away from the presence of these unwanted feelings. As a result, it can be beneficial to work with the other chapters in this book, such as self-esteem, low mood and anxiety, alongside this one.

The three-step process towards healthier anger

If anger was acknowledged as a natural and healthy emotion, I imagine it would bring about a big change in society. If we know that it's OK to want something but we don't always get it, we're less likely to try to obtain it through power. If we know it's acceptable to stand up for ourselves, we would learn assertiveness rather than passiveness or aggression. There are books written about how we could have world peace if everybody owned their anger. People wouldn't need to pick an argument with someone else in order to release what's repressed inside of them. Instead, they'd acknowledge and express their anger in a healthy way.

If the person in the example above was more comfortable with their anger, they might be able to see things from a different perspective. They would be able to see that the issue is not down to them as a person but, it is instead caused by their denial of their anger. Further denial leads to further repression of anger. This doesn't help but makes it worse instead, as it's storing up even more repressed anger in the pan. If they could see this and accept that anger is part of being human, they'd be able to work with it more consciously and find a healthier expression. They'd acknowledge their anger, work with it and find it much easier to control. They'd reduce the likelihood of these 'small' events affecting them. Even if they did, they'd understand them for what they were – the final straw triggering the release of unexpressed emotion in the pan. The pan would also have less repressed emotion in it if they're able to acknowledge and work to release it in a healthy way. Let's now explore a way that you can do this.

In an ideal world, you'd notice you're feeling angry, acknowledge the feeling, reflect on what it's telling you and find a way to express this safely. To help you do this, it's helpful to find a way to bring space into the process, to pause for a while and take time out. When you're on automatic, it's hard to stop anger escalating into an unhelpful situation. Here are three steps to help you do this.

1. Understand yourself
2. Pause before action
3. Respond healthily

Step 1: Understand yourself

First, remind yourself that you're a human being and anger is an essential part of that. It's natural to feel upset about hurting your toe. If you imagined people were laughing at you, it's understandable you felt angry about it. Remember this is your perspective though and not necessarily the truth. Sometimes people laugh when they see someone tripping over, but not always in an unkind way. Understanding what's being triggered in you gives you the opportunity to understand yourself. The following exercise will help you to do this. The more you understand, the more you'll feel able to control how it comes across to others.

Exercise 21: Understanding your anger

Write down some recent situations where you've felt angry.

- How does your anger manifest – shouting, withdrawing, tears, denial, sarcasm, self-loathing?
- What physical signs indicate that you're starting to feel angry – going red, an increase in pulse/heart rate, wanting to kick out, wanting to run?
- Can you identify what happens just before you express your anger to others? (This awareness could help you to prevent escalation in future scenarios.)
- What triggers your anger? Some examples:
- Do you feel misunderstood or victimized by someone or something and your anger is an expression of this?
- Do you feel threatened by another person or situation and your anger is a way of protecting yourself?
- Do you feel that life is out of control and your anger is a way of trying to regain that sense of control?
- Do you feel guilty for something and your anger is a way of deflecting this, as guilt can be a hard feeling to experience?
- Are you fearful of something and anger is a way of deflecting from this?
- Are you upset about the way you've been treated and your anger is an expression of this?
- Do you feel that you're unnoticed by others and your anger is a way of getting attention or respect from others?
- Are you upset that things didn't work out your way?
- Do you feel frustrated that your point of view wasn't considered or the outcome wasn't what you wanted?
- Are there any other reasons?

How effective is your way of being angry? Consider the impact on yourself and others, does it do its job? For example, you want to feel respected but you can see how others lose respect when you're shouting. Or they can't hear you as you do not assert yourself at all.

Remember that anger isn't a problem in itself unless it leads to physical or aggressive verbal outbursts that harm another person. Equally, if it is having a negative impact on you in any way, then working with your anger can be beneficial and prevent greater problems.

Always seek help from a professional if this is having a major impact on yourself or another, if your behaviour has become violent or you feel yourself or somebody else may be at risk of harm.

Step 2: Pause before action

Now that you have acknowledged you 'do' anger in some form, let's explore how pausing can help. Have you ever sent an angry email on the spur of the moment and then regretted doing it the next day? Have you upset somebody with an outburst where you said something you didn't really mean? If so, you're in the majority. This has happened to everyone at some point. If it happens frequently, building in a pause will help.

When you recognize that you're starting to feel angry – by showing signs of stress and irritation, feeling yourself going red or any other symptom – try to instigate some time out. Responding from a place of anger allows the situation to escalate. Pausing allows you some cool off time. So acknowledge the anger building up and remove yourself from the situation. Take a walk, do some exercise, be in nature, anything to give yourself a breather. Taking deep breaths, distracting yourself, learning techniques for relaxation and managing stress may also help you to navigate your timeout.

Going back to the injured toe, you might recognize that when you feel pain, you typically feel the need to lash out. You were embarrassed by falling over and hated it when you felt you were being laughed at. It felt as though the whole world was against you at that moment. You know that such scenarios always triggers your anger. You also have physical clues as you start to get hot, go red in the face, and feel tingling and pressure building up. By making this conscious, you can recognize future situations as they're arising and develop a plan to have a different outcome. You could carry on walking away from the situation or take yourself somewhere where you can comfortably take some deep breaths. Try to walk away from the situation without making any comment. You can always choose to bring up the health and safety issue or speak to your friends about how they reacted at a later date.

It might help to have some phrases on hand to help you walk away. For example, 'I'm going to take a break and catch up with you later', 'I need some time out', 'I'm going to have a walk and think this through', 'I'm not happy about the situation but think it's better if we talk later.' You'll need to find what feels comfortable for you. If you're in a situation where somebody is behaving inappropriately or unfairly towards you, you might set a boundary: "'It's not OK for me' or 'There's no need to speak to me like that' – but try to limit this to a phrase and then walk away. You may find you can still stand there using breathing or distraction. Be careful not to get drawn in, as one angry comment leads to another and before you know it, the situation has escalated. Acknowledge to yourself that your assertiveness and ability to be calm is likely to be respected by others. Aggression and anger are not. It takes strength and courage as well as patience and skill to walk away.

Passive-assertiveness-aggression continuum

Equally, a lack of anger when it's appropriate can potentially be as big an issue as too much anger. Processing your feelings of anger and how you feel generally might help you to find some healthy anger. Whenever you feel misunderstood, unfairly treated, left out or that your point of view has not

been considered, you have a right to your opinion, your
boundaries and to be treated respectfully. It's okay to say,
'It's not OK, you've upset me', 'That's not fair,' and so on.
If it's hard for you to say any of these things, building your
self-esteem may help.

A common misconception is that assertiveness may
come across as being aggressive. If you imagine a scale
from A–Z, at A you have complete compliance. You never
show any anger. People are unaware of your boundaries
and what's OK for you. Subconsciously, you give the
message it's acceptable to walk all over you and maybe
not respect you. At Z, you have aggression and are easily
tipped into showing your anger. In this place, it's hard
to hear your message among the noise. A dog that keeps
barking constantly loses its impact. If it barks too often,
you'll probably ignore it or not respond straight away.
Assertiveness is somewhere in the middle. N is between
A and Z. It's a healthier place. You stand up for yourself
where it's appropriate. Your message is more likely to be
heard and respected from this place.

Many people fear if they move from A, they'll become
aggressive (nearer Z). The reality is that taking steps towards
healthy anger will move you steadily towards N. It will take
a lot of movement before you're considered aggressive. The
next chapter on improving relationships can help you with
communication.

Step 3: Respond healthily

Now you've removed yourself away from the situation
and acknowledged your anger, you need an outlet. This
enables you to release the intensity of the feeling. This
can be equally valid with other emotions. It also gives you
some extra reflection time. One of the following may be
helpful:

- Do something active, such as gardening, martial arts, exercise (e.g. running, swimming, the gym, boxing), going for a walk in nature, jumping up and down on the spot.
- Draw/paint/write/play an instrument/do something creative that helps you to express how you're feeling, like drumming in the park, listening to music that resonates with your mood.
- Talk to somebody not involved in the situation who might be able to hear your anger and will also give you an objective point of view.
- Crying can also be a release for anger.
- Write down your angry thoughts. You can address them to either a person or the situation, or you can just write. It can be helpful to burn this at the end or bury it. If you're burning it, make sure that you do so safely. If you're responding to an email, write the email and then save it as a draft (remove the person's address temporarily from the top to remove any chance of it being sent prematurely). Decide on a different day if you need to send a message and if you do, update your draft from a calmer place.

Each of these activities allows the full impact of your anger to be released in a healthy way, i.e. you're not impacting on anyone else negatively or repressing the feeling. In the process, you may glean some understanding of how you feel. What has been triggered? What do you need to do, if anything, to feel better about the situation? You might like to revisit and reflect on the questions in understanding your anger in Exercise 21 earlier in this chapter. You'll hopefully be feeling much calmer and have more clarity. An additional perspective on the situation.

You now have a choice as to how to respond. You may wish to talk to the person involved. If you do so from a calm place, they're more likely to hear you as they're not on the defensive. You're also more likely to be clearer in what you say without the noise. If someone has upset you, your conversation creates an opportunity for something different in the future. You're setting an important boundary about what's not okay for you. It might be that working on the system or a process will help you. For example, if you're feeling overwhelmed by work and not getting the support of your manager, in addition to speaking to your manager, it might be worth exploring changes in the organization, such as how work is organized, the appraisal system, training and so on.

Alternatively, you may not feel the need to communicate anything having utilized a healthy outlet for your anger. You might choose to behave differently, opt to avoid certain dynamics or people or decide you need support from someone. If you feel there's injustice or you feel misunderstood, you might find it beneficial to get involved in causes in order to channel your passion, e.g. human rights, animal welfare, environmental campaigns, etc.

Understanding how your stories affect anger

You can influence how often you're triggered into anger by addressing your stories. The stories we tell ourselves impact our interpretation of situations. This, in turn, affects how we feel and what we do about it. Being conscious of the stories, allows you to check their validity. This may help to reduce the number of triggers you experience in the first place. It might be helpful to refer back to Chapter 3, if you need a reminder but remember that your stories contain assumptions and limiting beliefs. For example, you may be feeling misunderstood and unappreciated. You believe your parents, partner or flatmates are always criticising you for what you've not done around the house. They never notice the good things you do. Your teacher or boss constantly criticizes your work. You feel there's no point trying any more as they're just looking for you to make a mistake.

The impact of this belief is that it becomes the story you see. You're likely to expect it and go into situations on the defence: 'Everyone's against me.' As a result, you're critical or moody as you walk into the room. Your head is down. You stop doing anything around the house or trying with your work. If anyone asks you anything, you shrug your shoulders. You're either withdrawn and aloof or ready to bite their head off. Your reaction's understandable. It's not easy feeling like this. You're hurt. Frustrated. Yet, it's also important to explore how your behaviour might be self-fulfilling. Your defensiveness could be attracting criticism. Maybe your parents intended to praise you today but when you walked into the room with a scowl on your face, your arms folded and snapped at the first question they asked, your reaction made them forget it. They felt criticized, on the defensive and as a result, responded with more criticism.

If you're able to step back from the situation, you might be able to see the pattern at play. It's your interpretation of the situation that makes you feel misunderstood. Your parents may not openly give praise but they think it all the time. They may not realize how critically they're coming across. The dynamic between you is affecting the situation. Both chapters on relationships in this book might help you understand this more. Recognizing this may help to diffuse your feelings of anger. You might be able to communicate with them and find a different way or you might change your own behaviour. Acknowledging the hurt and finding an outlet for this will also help to diffuse the situation. Otherwise, the unresolved emotion builds up, creating a bigger issue.

Going back to the toe example, the story that seems to play out is that you're someone to laugh at. Maybe you get it wrong, are not taken seriously or you don't feel good enough. Maybe the story is that other people are always tripping you up in life and stopping you from achieving what you want. Whatever the story is, exploring the beliefs behind it and working on your anger and self-esteem, will help to reduce the intensity of the trigger in future. The more you accept your anger, the less scary it'll be. You'll also feel more in control. If anger is making your life difficult or you're finding it hard to work on your stories, try talking to somebody. It can be someone you trust or a professional. If your anger is becoming violent in any way, please also seek professional help.

What if you are the recipient of anger?

Everyone gets angry from time to time and it's natural to express this in front of or at loved ones occasionally. We all need to know that we can be stressed and be human in front of others and not be punished for it. This doesn't mean, however, that this should be frequent or in any way emotionally or physically abusive. If you're the recipient of any emotional or physical abuse, please do seek professional help. If your friend, relative or partner is very angry when communicating something to you, it's absolutely acceptable to ask them to calm down and release their emotion in a healthy way. Ask them to talk to you after they have done this so that you can hear their message more clearly and be able to respond more helpfully. There's more information about this in the next chapter.

Seeking professional help
Always seek professional help if your symptoms are affecting you severely over a longer period of time or if you or someone else is at risk of harm in any way. Also, seek help if you are the recipient or instigator of any emotional or physical abuse or if your anger is having a negative impact on you or another in any way.

Summary

○ All human beings – regardless of personality or type – experience feelings of anger from time to time.

○ Anger is essential in bringing about change, whether personally or on a bigger scale. We need to feel anger in order to know that we feel victimized, that there is injustice or that something is meaningful to us.

○ Anger can be over or underused if it is repressed or denied. We feel more in control of anger by understanding it, learning to pause and finding ways to express it safely.

○ Working on challenging our thinking and limiting beliefs can help to reduce any triggers of anger.

○ It's not about being perfect with anger as we will all 'blow a fuse' or say something we regret at some point. Being human is doing our best but accepting that sometimes we'll not be able to do this.

Chapter 9

IMPROVING RELATIONSHIPS WITH OTHERS

As we explored in Chapter 4, there's no such thing as a perfect relationship. All relationships include an element of upset and fallout. This is an inevitable part of being human. We all have emotions, make mistakes, get the wrong end of the stick, make assumptions, become stressed and react to others. When you're stressed or upset, you're most likely to take it out on those you're closest to. With most people, that's most likely to be a parent, a long-term partner or very close friend. It's 'safer' to do this as they're most likely to love you even for your 'bad' points. They'll still be there even when you're grumpy or shout occasionally.

When you face any difficulty in a relationship, it offers an opportunity for growth. Something to learn from. Reflecting and working on this can strengthen you as a person or enable the relationship to become stronger. In some relationships, this can mean it's time to move on. This is an inevitable part of life for everyone but facing this can be extremely difficult. Even with relationships that you know have run their course, endings are still upsetting. As anyone who's experienced heartbreak will know, it takes time to overcome endings and rebuild the inevitable loss of self-esteem. This chapter will help you to tackle relationship difficulties and identify what can help.

How can you improve your relationships?

When you face a difficulty in a relationship, remind yourself it's part of being human. It's not something you're doing wrong but rather an opportunity to learn something about yourself or your relationship. Let's consider three options to help you improve the relationship:

1. Communicate your needs/feedback about their behaviour.
2. Change your behaviour.
3. Accept the situation.

Let's look at each of these options in more depth in the following sections.

Option 1: Communicate your needs/ feedback about their behaviour

Let's explore this through the eyes of Jasmine. She's feeling irritated by her mum, who seems to constantly tell her what to do, what not to do when to do it and even how. What career she should be looking at, when to do her work, what she should cook for tea and so on. She feels her mum is trying to control what she does. It's hard to breathe. She feels suffocated and just wants her own space. She's old enough to make her own decisions. Why can't her mum see this? Why won't she get off her case? It's common to feel frustrated in a relationship. To want someone to stop or start doing something differently. Jasmine's not alone in this. What often happens is we assume the other person knows what we want. We assume it's obvious. This is a false assumption as other people aren't able to read your mind. If you can say what you need, you have a higher chance of it happening. The person may end up saying no, but at least you're not hoping for something to happen that never will. If you get a no, move to option 2 or 3. Let's consider some of the important communication principles that can help you get your message across.

Communicate the context

If you're going to share what's bothering you, it can be helpful to give some context. Without it, the person can go on the defensive and make it much harder for them to hear your message. Imagine saying to your mum, 'You're really annoying. All you do is control me. Please stop doing it.' She's likely to feel attacked and unappreciated. It's critical and hard to receive. If instead, you say something along the lines of: 'Mum, I really appreciate everything you do for me but I need to talk to you about something that's bothering me. Please could you listen to what I need to say so that we can find a way to improve the situation?' How much easier is that to hear? You'll need to find the words that feel comfortable for you. It's hard to do this when you're full of emotion. So before any communication, acknowledge what you're feeling, find an outlet and then consider what you need to say.

In a friendship or intimate relationship, try something along the lines of 'I really value our relationship. Can we talk about something that might prevent misunderstandings?' Imagine, instead, that your partner of two months starts to tell you they're unhappy about something. Without the context, you second-guess they're finishing the relationship. You're upset and immediately on the defensive. You're unlikely to hear what they're saying. In these scenarios, a misunderstanding or an argument is likely. The issues don't get resolved and could even get worse.

Focus on the behaviour

Providing specific feedback about someone else's behaviour is much more helpful than a comment about their character. Telling someone they're controlling or annoying is about their character rather than their behaviour. I understand where you're coming from, but feedback in this way is not helpful to hear and can easily lead to an argument. Remember, we're all annoying from time to time. We all make mistakes. Our behaviour isn't necessarily a reflection of who we are as a person. Showing anger doesn't necessarily make you an angry person. Doing something that's perceived by another as unkind doesn't make you an unkind person. It's more constructive to feedback the behaviour rather than the judgement, 'When you do x, it makes me feel annoyed' rather than 'You're so annoying.'

Be as specific as possible

Try to avoid generalizing and be as specific as possible with your examples. Rather than, "You always…' try to state a particular time. Jasmine might say, 'Yesterday you told me to get my work done and what I should cook for tea. I felt frustrated. I feel capable of making my own decisions about my work. I also had my own ideas for tea.' Any suggestions about what might help are also useful. 'Could you trust me to do my work when's best for me. I'm happy to give you an update but can we agree on what works for us both. Can we agree which days I'm cooking and then let me decide what to cook. Within reason, of course.' This kind of conversation is always better when you're not feeling angry.

Understand and acknowledge your part in the dynamic

In Chapter 4, we explored the idea that in any relationship, both parties are contributing to any dynamic.[1] When you accept you're part of the issue, change is more likely.

Otherwise, blame can be apportioned to the other person keeping you in a place of victim. Everyone else is at fault but not you. What might be your part in the dynamic? For Jasmine, what's contributing to her mum coming across as controlling? By discussing it with her, including what's behind her behaviour and what both of them could do to help the situation, it's likely to feel a much more productive conversation. They're both part of the solution.

Jasmine's mum might think she's not taking responsibility for her future and so has to prompt Jasmine to focus on this. By understanding both points of view, they agree on a way forward. Jasmine wants space to think about this in her own way, without constant prompts. Jasmine's mum wants to know there's a plan. They agree a different approach to meet both of their needs. With regard to cooking, Jasmine understands her mum goes food shopping on a particular day and so the menu is planned for the week. Jasmine agrees to either give her mum her ingredients list in advance or buy the ingredients herself.

The body as a source of information

In all relationships, it's helpful to be aware of your needs. Try to check in with yourself frequently so that you're able to answer questions such as these:

- How comfortable are you with this suggestion?
- What clues is your body giving you?
- How are your energy levels?
- Do you want to go out tonight or do you need to rest? If you do go out, where would you like to go? With who? If you decide to rest, what would nourish you the most?
- Are you comfortable with the way you're being spoken to?
- What is your truth? Do you speak your truth or what you imagine others want to hear?

- What are your aspirations and passions? Do you follow them or what others want or expect you to do?
- How comfortable are you in this relationship (intimate or friendship)? Do you feel able to be yourself? Does the relationship feel healthy to you? Do you feel respected? Do you want to have sex right now? In this way? With this person? On these terms?

When we're familiar with answers like these and can listen to the clues from our body, it's much easier to be authentic. Regular practice of Guided Meditation 10 – Body Awareness Scan in Chapter 13 – can help you answer these questions. Also Exercise 19 on decision making in Chapter 7 could also be helpful.

Option 2: Change your behaviour

If you keep ordering the same things, that's what you'll get. If you want something different, you need to change your order. It is exactly the same in relationships. Our behaviour can fall into unhelpful patterns. If Jasmine continues to expect to cook what she wants on the day, without prior arrangement, it's unlikely to happen. Equally, if she doesn't show signs of planning her future, her mum's likely to continue asking her about it. By changing our own behaviour, we can influence the behaviour of someone else. You don't necessarily have to carry out option 1 in conjunction with this.

Let's imagine you speak to your parents weekly on the phone. Most of the conversation is with your mum because your dad seems to find it hard to discuss anything over the phone. He never asks how you are or what's going on for you. Your phone conversations last less than a minute before you're passed onto your mum. You feel frustrated by this. You're becoming more frustrated by each phone call. You're feeling down and if you can't tell him anything generally, how can you tell him this?

You try option 2. You reflect on your relationship with your dad. You consider the broader picture. What does your dad's behaviour say about him? Why does his behaviour bother you? What feelings does it provoke? What are your assumptions and conclusions? What story are you interpreting? What's your part in the dynamic? Is there any other information that might be helpful? You decide to speak to your mum and brother about it. They help you realize it's just the way he is. He doesn't particularly like talking on the phone. It's not personal to you. He's like it with everyone. This is reassuring to you as you realize deep down you were worrying that your dad didn't care about you. You look at the evidence he does care and realize he shows his love in a different way. He always does lots for you practically which is more comfortable for him than words.

You can also see that you're already wound up when you're on the phone to your dad, expecting him not to ask you anything. You respond with short answers and realize he may be picking up on this. This may contribute to how comfortable he feels on the phone. You could help him to feel more at ease through your behaviour. You could ask your dad how he is and what he's up to. You could tell him something about your day rather than expecting him to ask. Maybe he's interested but doesn't know how to ask. Maybe he doesn't want to pry. You also decide to spend some time with your dad face-to-face. You decide to show your dad some affection which might help him to reciprocate.

Working on yourself

In Chapters 3 and 4, we explored how our beliefs and stories are reinforced by mirroring and how we collect evidence. For this reason, the more you work on yourself, the better your relationships. Gandhi said, 'Be the change you want to be.' If you want a more loving relationship, you need to start by loving yourself. If you want more peace, then make peace with yourself. If you want more fun, take yourself less seriously. You'll start to notice a difference in others in response to your changes. It might be helpful to do this in conjunction with the chapter on attracting new positive beliefs and stories. It might also be helpful to consider some of the ideas we've already explored in this book. What steps could you address regarding yourself that might strengthen your relationships? Possible options include:

- Nonattachment to the outcome – when we're fixated on something working out in a particular way, we create pressure and tension. This can be picked up by the other person who won't feel comfortable. It can also prevent you from being yourself.
- Ensure balance in your life. Have a good repertoire of people and activities – see also Chapters 1 and 14.
- Ensure you have a healthy emotional outlet so that no one relationship is taking the brunt of this – see also Chapter 2.
- Happiness comes from within and is a process – what can you do to make yourself happy rather than relying on your relationship to do so? See also Chapter 1.
- Being aware of your defences and unhelpful coping strategies – what might be preventing this relationship? See also Chapters 2 and 4.
- Stories affect how we interpret situations and can be self-fulfilling – what's playing out in your relationships? What stories can you work on to improve your relationships? See also Chapters 3 and 4.
- Self-esteem – how confident and secure do you feel in yourself? See also Chapter 7.

This list is not intended to feel like a lot of hard work. We all have stuff to work on. Be kind to yourself and acknowledge this. Identify one thing that could help right now. Work on that first before tackling anything else. In a few months, you could work on something else or, when something comes up in one of your relationships, revisit the list and this chapter.

Option 3: Accept the situation

Every relationship will involve behaviours that irritate the other person. For example, housemates not tidying up after themselves, or siblings leaving wet towels on the floor. These little things can become very frustrating. You might have asked them to not do it (option 1) but it's had little or no effect. This issue, while only a small thing, is leading you to feel unappreciated and put on. If you explore this story of feeling unappreciated, you might recognize the assumptions. While it's annoying, it's not proof they don't care about you. Maybe the person just forgets, it's a habit, they're trying really hard to remember or they don't see it in the same way as you.

Consider the pros and cons of the situation. Generally, how is the relationship? Is this the only thing that bothers you? Looking at the bigger picture, you might remember all their positive points. You have a choice. You can carry on trying to change the situation and feel frustrated or you could accept the situation for what it is. You might decide the overall picture is worth it. You could laugh about the situation and just ignore the mess, accepting they'll deal with it in their own time. Or you could take a few minutes to tidy up while thinking about the things they do for you. Remember, there are likely to be lots of things you do that irritates them. Or you could decide it's too big a deal for you and walk away.

In any relationship, there'll be things that won't change. Your partner doesn't want to change their diet or stop seeing a particular friend. Your friends aren't into clubbing as much as you. You don't want to drink every time you go out. You don't want to spend as much money as the others or go to the same places. We all have different levels of energy, cleanliness, tidiness, and we all have different ways of doing things. We can try to get someone else to change but sometimes we have to accept people for who they are – a unique human with their own beliefs, strengths and opportunity areas. They may not want to change or are not able to, even if they wanted to. There's no such thing as a person that can meet all of your needs. Maybe they're a good listener and always there for you or they make you laugh but you couldn't live with them.

It can be helpful to look at a relationship over a period of time rather than at isolated incidents to ensure that you're not reacting to a one-off or a phase. People have periods of their life where they're going through difficulties and we may need to be more understanding and patient. It can be helpful to talk to someone about your feelings or find an outlet for them. This can help to prevent a build-up of resentment and frustration. We can't easily walk away from all relationships. If that is the case, seek help and support.

You really care for your girlfriend but find the amount of time she spends playing hockey difficult. Weighing up the situation, you might decide it's important to keep the relationship but stop putting pressure on it to change. Rather than assuming her devotion to hockey reflects her feelings towards you, you decide instead to spend time with your own hobbies. You accept the situation and choose how best to focus your time and attention. Alternatively, you could walk away from the relationship. You might respect her love of sport but decide it's incompatible with the amount of time and energy you'd like from a relationship.

Which option should I choose?

There may be one option that's most appropriate to your situation or you might find all could be of benefit. If this is the case, prioritize them in order of preference. Make sure that you give sufficient time for something to work before trying a further option. You might also like to practice communicating with a friend or writing down key points to help you. There's no right or wrong. As human beings, we learn through our experiences. Let's go back to Molly and Rob in Chapter 4 to explore how the options could work out in practice.

Molly's insecure about her relationship with Rob because she's been hurt in the past and this is affecting their relationship. She's anxious the relationship will fail so is spending lots of time with Rob and trying to please him. She always goes along with his suggestions and makes plans based on what she thinks he'd like to do. This also ensures he's spending time with her rather than noticing any other potential girlfriends. Rob is getting frustrated by Molly always saying yes. He senses deep down that she doesn't want to do the things he chooses. He'd rather watch his local sports team just with his mates as he knows they're into it too. He's also missing spending time with them on his own. Rob and Molly are starting to argue more and more. Rob is requesting more time with his friends alone. Molly's unhappy about this and realizes she needs to do something about it.

So in option 1, Molly might tell Rob she's afraid of getting hurt. She feels insecure about his feelings towards her. She's worried that his decision to spend time with his friends is because he doesn't really want to spend time with her. She tells him it would be helpful if he told her how he feels and gave some context around his decisions. It would also be helpful to hear that his decision to spend time with his friends is not related to him wanting to end the relationship. By opening this dialogue, Molly and Rob are able to talk about the dynamic between them and agree on what will help them both. They agree when they'll spend time together doing things they both enjoy. Molly understands Rob's need to spend time with his friends and realizes that she would benefit from doing the same.

Following option 2, Molly might recognize her insecurity is related to her past relationships. Her relationship with Rob is not necessarily the same as her past relationships. She can see the story she's formed and how this is affecting her behaviour with Rob. Molly recognizes that by spending too much time with him and over-pleasing, she may actually bring about a breakup, the situation she fears. She decides to work on this story and focus on building happiness within herself. As a result, she gives the relationship more space. They spend less time together but it's a much happier time as they're both more relaxed. She's less insecure about him seeing more of his friends. Molly's also happier in herself after spending time with other people as well. She realizes Rob's request for space was reasonable and healthy.

Molly might go to option 3 if the first two options don't work, or she may go straight there. Molly has a choice whether or not to accept Rob's need for space. If she genuinely accepts it's a good thing, her feelings of sadness and insecurity will dissipate. Or she may choose to end the relationship and find someone who she feels is compatible with the amount of time she wishes to spend with her partner. This may be difficult in the short term but could bring her more happiness in the long run. The 'watch out' in this scenario is that if Molly doesn't work on her insecurities, they may play out in her next relationship. It's always worth working on yourself, but you always have a choice as to whether you stay in a relationship or move on.

What if you're the recipient of any difficulty?

So far, we've explored relationships where you're the instigator of change. What happens if you're on the receiving end? Hopefully, the information in the rest of chapter is still helpful but let's look at some additional points.

Try to stay neutral

If someone brings up a disagreement with you and they're expressing their anger, hurt or frustration, it can be really difficult to hear this. Especially if they're not following the communication principles outlined in this chapter. You may hear some hurtful things and retaliate in defence. This is especially true if you have experienced being hurt by others before. The natural tendency is to shout back. We're all human. The argument can then escalate and become a much bigger thing. You lose sight of the message. If you're able to stay calm and try to listen to their message without reacting, it would benefit you both. You'd see that they're feeling hurt and trying to communicate something to you. Try to understand their point of view even if you don't agree with what's being said. It's highly appropriate to suggest delaying the conversation until they're calm. You could share with them the communication principles from this chapter.

Golden bubble

If you're facing difficulties in a relationship or feeling targeted by others, it can sometimes feel as though you're taking on the hurt physically. Sometimes name-calling can be described by children as something they feel. It can help to imagine the golden bubble that's mentioned in each meditation. Imagine this being all around you as a protective bubble that shields you from the words and feelings of others. Imagine them bouncing off the side and falling to the floor.

Facing endings

My heart goes out to anyone who's facing an ending of any kind. It can be excruciating, even heartbreaking. You didn't spot it coming. You don't want it. You can't imagine a happy life without this person in it. You need time and space to come to terms with this. You'll face natural cycles of not wanting to face it and trying to fight it, as well as sadness and loss of what you had, what you expected to have in future and the painful exploration of why it may have happened. You may also experience anger towards them, yourself or life in general. You're also likely to have a dip in confidence and self-esteem. It's really important to have a good support network around you. People you can talk to. People who will care for you and help you to stay healthy. You might not want to cook or eat the right things. You may be tempted by unhealthy coping strategies. You'll also need an outlet for your emotions. Take the time you need and seek support as you adjust to coming to terms with the ending. It can take weeks, months and sometimes longer. We're all different.

Try to be yourself

While at university, I read about the Abilene Paradox, which was illustrated by a story about a grandad whose family was visiting him for the day.[2] Over the phone, they asked him what he'd like to do. He suggested visiting a local attraction as he thought they'd like to do that. His preference was to stay at home but he felt he should offer something more exciting. After all, they were travelling all that way. At this suggestion, his family groaned inwardly. After driving a long way to see him, the last thing they wanted to do was get back in the car. Assuming this was what he wanted though, they felt they should go along with it. They didn't think he got out often and wanted to give him the opportunity. Who do you think had a good time? While everyone was glad to see each other, nobody truly enjoyed the excursion.

The moral of the Abilene Paradox is to try to be as authentic as possible. When someone asks you what you'd like to do, try to respond as honestly as you can. When we're not authentic about what we want or try to be somebody we're not, another part of us is unfulfilled or sad. Of course, we can't always get our way and compromise is sometimes appropriate, but it helps to know our own feelings. If you don't know them, take steps to find out. Remember Exercise 19 on decision-making in Chapter 7. It's much easier in a relationship if you can trust what the other person is saying. Personally, I have to know that someone is OK to say no to me before I'll ask them a favour.

Find 'your tribe'

We all deserve to be with people who treat us with respect. Where we feel happy and can be ourselves. Remember back to Chapter 4 and the section on healthy relationships? If you don't feel respected or happy, find the person/group of people where you do. It can be a very scary thought to leave a relationship. You may fear the unknown or that there's no one else out there. This is understandable but it's not a reason to be unhappy. Look out for other people, try different things, connect with others who are like you.

Guided Meditation 6 at the end of this chapter is my version of a well-known loving-kindness practice. Research has shown that regular usage of this meditation can have significant benefits on wellbeing and relationships, not just immediately but also in the longer term.[3] You can use this to help your relationship with yourself, relationships that are already positive with others, relationships where there are conflicts or difficulties and also your relationship with this planet.

Seek professional help

If you're experiencing any emotional or physical abuse or in any way worried that you or another are at risk of harm, please do seek professional help.

Guided Meditation 6: Loving Kindness[3]

This guided meditation will help you to improve your relationship with yourself and others.

natalieread.online/kindness

Summary

○   There are three options to help improve your relationships: communicate your needs/feedback their behaviour, change yourself or accept the situation.

○   If you're communicating a message, it can be helpful to state the context; be specific, focus only on the behaviour rather than their character and acknowledge the part you play in the dynamic.

○   It can help to look at yourself, address your happiness, confidence and self-esteem, as well as the challenging stories and beliefs that affect your relationships.

○   Exploring the bigger picture can help you determine whether to accept the situation as it is or walk away.

○   Endings can be extremely difficult so finding support, an emotional outlet and being kind to yourself is important.

○   If you're the recipient of a relationship difficulty, try to stay neutral and avoid making assumptions. Utilize the golden bubble image to protect yourself, tap into your body as a source of information for what's right for you and seek support from others.

Part III

EMBRACING CHANGE AND LIVING WITH HAPPINESS

Chapter 10

BUILDING RESILIENCE TO OVERCOME DIFFICULTIES

Resilience is a hot topic at the moment that is mentioned in many corporate vision statements and has featured in many competency frameworks. Employers are looking for it. Educational organizations strive to support students in developing it. The number of blogs and books on the subject is increasing. Why? Because we all need it. Whether you know it or not, resilience can make a difference in life and can help you personally and professionally in all aspects of life. We're all human and face a mixture of happy times and periods where life feels tough. Resilience can help you cope with these tougher periods and feel more able to overcome them. In this chapter, we'll explore what resilience is, evaluate your level of resilience and identify how to strengthen it further.[1]

What is resilience?

Resilience is the ability to bounce back and recover from life's difficulties. It doesn't mean you enjoy the difficulty but you recognize that it's simply part of life. With resilience, you're more likely to spot change or difficulty, so you can proactively manage it. Even if the change takes you by surprise, you're more likely to respond to it quickly and more effectively. Being resilient means being able to draw on strategies to help you manage while trusting you'll get through it, so making it easier to navigate life's ups and downs. With resilience, you cope with change and overcome setbacks more easily. While some people are naturally more resilient than others, the good news is that everybody can develop and strengthen resilience. Somebody with higher resilience is more likely to believe:

- Life is full of ups and downs.
- Difficulties pass.
- Emotions come and go.
- Despite appearances, difficulties affect everybody.
- It's human to make mistakes.
- Everybody has strengths and development areas.
- You're not to blame for your problems.
- Judgements are assumptions and not necessarily the truth.
- No one's perfect. Life's not perfect. We're all human.
- Asking for help is a sign of strength, not weakness.
- Overcoming difficulties makes you stronger.
- Difficulties are opportunities to learn or grow or help you change direction.
- It's not possible to be liked by everybody.
- If I'm rejected, the person or situation was not right for me. Something or somebody else is more suitable.

Why is resilience important?

Someone with less resilience may not spot the difficulty and ignore it (consciously or subconsciously), which can prolong it or make it bigger. Imagine a relationship difficulty. Deep down, you know the relationship isn't healthy or working out anymore. You can't bear to acknowledge this, as the thought of change is too frightening. Maybe you're not allowing yourself to face it. We're all prone to this to some degree, resilient or not. Someone with more resilience won't let this go on for too long. They know facing up to problems is important, are less likely to take it personally and more able to draw on the support they need to overcome it. Having resilience makes it easier (but not easy) to face your difficulties. Remember resistance adds additional layers of emotion making the problem harder to overcome.

Building more resilience not only helps increase your quota of happiness, self-esteem, relationships and productivity, but can also help with your studies, work and make you more attractive to an employer. When I started my graduate job, one of the competencies desired and measured was 'coping with change'. Change was defined as something you had to face occasionally. Being able to proactively deal with change or lead new change was desired. By the time I left the organization 10 years later, the competency was renamed 'agility'. The new focus was managing and leading constant change and this reflected the global speed of change. Change was no longer an occasional thing but something inevitable and ongoing. I believe this change of pace has continued. How much political change have we faced in the past year alone? Technology is constantly changing. Weather patterns are arguably more severe. To cope with these changes, we need to be flexible and adaptable, two important components of resilience.

Exercise 22: Evaluate your level of resilience

How resilient are you? You're probably more resilient than you think. Anyone that's experienced change in their life will have some level of resilience. Exercise 1 on resilience in Chapter 1 may help you see this. Below are a number of different components that are important for resilience. Consider each of them, in turn, giving yourself a mark out of 10 (0 = no skill, 10 = excellent skill). You may spot some strengths and other areas that you could improve on.

Areas of resilience	Rating out of 10	Action to develop or strengthen further
Self-awareness: How often do you take time to monitor your stress levels, energy levels, productivity, level of happiness, feelings, needs and preferences?		
Self-reflection: How often do you review situations/relationships in your life? What's working? What's needing attention? What's being triggered? What are you learning about yourself?		
Self-care regime: How well do you take care of yourself to ensure happiness, balance, relaxation, fun? How healthy and effective are your coping strategies?		
Stress management: How effective is your ability to monitor your stress levels. What level is comfortable? What preventative steps do you take to manage stress and promote relaxation? What signs indicate that you're struggling to cope? What helps you reduce overwhelm?		

Continued

Areas of resilience	Rating out of 10	Action to develop or strengthen further
Self-compassion: How kindly do you speak to yourself? When you face difficulty, how self-compassionate are you? How often do you focus on your strengths and positive qualities rather than dwell on issues?		
Problem solving: How proactive are you in acknowledging any difficulty versus a tendency to procrastinate or avoid situations? How effective is your ability to overcome problems and learn from them?		
Support network: How often do you connect with different groups of people in a meaningful way? Do you have a repertoire of people who can provide support? How willing are you to ask for help?		
Broaden your perspective: How often do you take a step back or take an outside view of your situation? What assumptions limit your perspective?		

In the following sections, we'll look at each area in more detail.

Developing self-awareness

How can you make self-awareness part of your daily routine? It's hard to overcome setbacks in life if you're not aware of them. Do you know when you're unhappy? Frustrated?

Stressed? Overwhelmed? Out of your depth? Imagine yourself as a rechargeable battery. Experiencing each of these feelings will drain the energy in your battery. It's important to know how much energy is used up, what depletes your energy, what recharges it and when to recharge. It's possible to go into the 'red' for a short period of time but it's not advisable for long periods. Doing this could lead to lowered immunity and even burnout.

The more you can learn to recognize the clues your body gives you, the quicker you can respond. If you're not aware, you can't action anything. If you're not used to tuning into your feelings or you've avoided them, practising self-awareness is important. You can develop this by taking time each day to do one of the following. Using Guided Meditation 10 – Body Awareness Scan (see Chapter 13), writing down your thoughts and feelings, breathing deeply, walking in nature or talking with friends. Many of the exercises in this book can also help you to develop self-awareness.

Taking time for self-reflection

Self-reflection is an important step to enable self-awareness. It's helpful to review what's going on in your life and take steps to address things proactively. This helps you anticipate and come to terms with situations more readily. Identifying situations that aren't working and exploring options that can help you improve them, identifying triggers and stories and taking steps to work on them. Doing the exercises in this book and taking the time to read it is another opportunity for self-reflection. The more you do this, the more your chance of happiness and avoiding repetitive scenarios.

Practising self-care

We all know the importance of self-care in theory but don't necessarily follow it through into practice. Having good self-care not only provides the benefits of looking after yourself, there are also benefits in the process, as you will feel good about looking after yourself. With good self-care, you'll be more productive, happier in yourself and able to move forwards towards your goals. A friend of mine heard a talk by a professional sportsman who believed the most important day in his training schedule was the day he rested – when his muscles fully integrated the impact of the training schedule throughout the week.

When you're experiencing change, it's important to evaluate your self-care. When you leave home, start a new job, become involved in a new relationship, it can help to notice what's worked in the past. Noticing you work best in a quiet environment, benefit from walking in nature, feel overwhelmed if you've not had a certain level of exercise or like an active social life can be helpful to know. In the new environment, making a conscious effort to reapply these factors will help you to adjust. Here's a questionnaire to evaluate your level of self-care. It's intended to be thought-provoking rather than definitive.

Exercise 23: Self-care questionnaire
Consider each sentence below and make a note of whether you agree, disagree or are neutral in your response.

- I make time for exercise several times a week.
- I drink lots of fluids daily (excluding alcohol, sugary drinks and caffeine).
- I have a healthy diet daily (lots of fruit and vegetables, balance of food groups, limited processed and junk food).

- I have a good quantity of quality sleep most nights.
- I know when I'm stressed and take steps to release it.
- I know what I'm feeling most of the time.
- I have a healthy outlet for my feelings.
- I do things that make me feel happy at least several times a week.
- I spend time on my own several times a week.
- I do things that make me feel relaxed several times a week.
- I spend time in nature several times a week.
- I focus on my strengths several times a week.
- I am more positive than negative about life.
- I do things that have meaning for me several times a week.
- I work on myself and have reflection time regularly.
- I spend time with a variety of friends, family members and other people who care about me regularly.
- I have a healthy balance between work and play.
- I devote time to considering my future regularly.
- I reach out for support when I need it.
- I drink alcohol socially and within health guidelines.
- I avoid drugs and smoking.
- My workspace is separate from my sleeping space.
- I avoid electronic gadgets and wind down at least an hour before sleeping.
- I take time to eat my meals and allow myself to digest my food properly.
- I feel I'm able to take life at a pace that is comfortable for me. I only occasionally rush around and feel stressed.

Identify from your list the steps that you could take to improve your self-care. If you have any unhealthy coping strategies, identify the need they fulfil. Could you meet this need in a healthier way? For example, if eating junk food makes you feel good about yourself, could you use exercise instead? Note, when facing a difficult or stressful phase, you may need to increase your level of self-care.

Using stress management

Being able to recognize when you're feeling stressed and taking steps to bring your body back into balance is important. We discussed how the fight-or-flight response impacts the body and the importance of exercise and relaxation in Chapter 6 and this chapter can help you with managing overwhelm. A good self-care regime also helps with stress management. It's important to spot the signs that indicate your stress levels are becoming too high and your ability to address this. You can also improve your stress levels by creating a more nurturing environment with the following:

- Increasing the time spent on activities that nourish you, e.g. time in nature, listening to positive music, meditation, watching/reading positive TV and books.
- Reducing the time spent on activities that deplete you, e.g. TV/books with fear/violence, electronic gadgets, ruminating on negative emotions and thoughts.
- Creating a positive environment to live and work in – clear and decluttered, with plants and flowers, etc.
- Positive influences – surrounding yourself with people who support you and your wellbeing, positive role models.

Having self-compassion

When you face difficulty, berating yourself only adds to the problem. Are you a perfectionist? Do you expect too much of yourself? Do you tend to overwork? Do you procrastinate? Are you overly self-critical? While these are all natural responses, learning to give yourself self-compassion instead will be much more helpful. So when things are stressful or not working out as you had hoped, allow yourself a good cry, take some time out, have a relaxing bath, and spend time with friends and family that care about you. Tell yourself you're doing the best you can and everyone experiences difficulties. It's difficult to have an objective perspective when you're in the middle of something. Giving yourself time for self-care and self-compassion allows you to express the feeling and look after yourself. Thereafter is usually a good time to seek perspective. You might also want to refer to Chapter 7 on self-esteem and Chapter 12 on the path to self-love for further ideas.

Problem-solving

Recognizing there's a problem is usually the first step towards solving it. Once you've acknowledged this, you can decide what to do next.

Exercise 24: Finding a way forwards[2]

Use this self-coaching tool to help you find a way forwards through a problem.

Goal

- What would you like to achieve/be different?
- How would your life be if you did achieve this goal?
- How will you know when you've achieved this?
- Is it worth going for?

Try to make this goal or outcome as specific as you can. Also check how realistic this is, as well as how it fits in with your other priorities. Is it possible for you to achieve this? Does something else need to give? It's important that it's motivational for you to do this. Considering what the difference it will make to your life can help you to create motivation. If you're not feeling excited about it or that it has a level of importance, it's unlikely you'll succeed.

Context

- Where are you now versus your goal?
- What successes or failures have you had that would be helpful to learn from?
- Are there any blocks?

It's helpful to be honest with yourself about anything that may have got in the way in the past; otherwise, the issue may arise again. Facing it head-on will help your chances of success. If you can identify whether the block is at a skill level or is about confidence, resources, belief, anxiety or fear, perfectionism, lack of motivation, distractions, etc, means you may be able to put something in place to overcome this.

Possibilities

- What different options are there?
- What else?
- What has been tried in the past? What does research say?
- What are the advantages and disadvantages of each option?

The more options that you can come up with, the better the solution. It might be helpful to imagine there are no limits so that you can consider a wide range of options. If there were unlimited resources, with no financial or time constraints, et cetera, what would you do? Then consider what would you do if there were limits. Sometimes we limit ourselves without realising it and so can miss out on a possible solution.

Action

- Which solution offers the best chance of success?
- What support do you need to help you?
- What difficulties might you need to overcome?
- What can you bring in to help address any block?
- How will you know if you have reached success?
- How often do you need to review your progress?

A problem that is broken into smaller chunks can be much easier to comprehend than one big one. It can also be helpful to evaluate what's within your control. If the problem is complex or there are unhealthy dynamics at play, you may need to get support from another person to tackle the issue. It can be beneficial anyway to have a sounding board or additional perspective.

Evaluation

*   How is your plan going? Are you on track? Is your solution working?
*   Do you need to make any amendments?
*   What support do you need?

Regular monitoring will help you progress. If all is going well, acknowledging your success will help you with your motivation to keep going. If things require some minor changes, doing this proactively will help to build confidence. If you're finding things aren't going to plan, acknowledge that this sometimes happens and revisit the process. You may need to get some extra advice or resources to help you. The sooner you do this, the better you'll feel. Remember, we all learn from experiences. The evaluation is more effective if done during the process, as well as afterwards.

How effective is your support network?

It helps to have a network of support and this can include friends and family, peers, tutors and teachers, colleagues, staff and friends from sports, hobbies, religious or spiritual groups and volunteering groups. It's not just being able to reach out when we need support. We feel a sense of connection when we're involved with others. Having connections with others brings the potential for happiness and wellbeing, as well as a sense of belonging, appreciation and validation. When we have a variety of people to choose from, it's easier to find someone who can:

- Be a shoulder to cry on
- Give us different perspectives on life
- Listen well
- Make you laugh
- Give you an honest opinion (How did you come across today? What outfit suits you best?)
- Accompany you when needed
- Participate in activities you love
- Encourage you to push yourself – in a good way

No one person can do everything so having a variety of people in your life is helpful. Remember, asking for help is a sign of strength and courage. You're saying to yourself, 'I'm important enough to take care of.' You're asking for what you need. When you do that, you also give permission to others to do the same. Sometimes you may need to seek help outside of your support network – maybe from a doctor, teacher, counsellor or other professional. Everyone faces difficulties in life, even your parents, headteacher, employer and celebrities. It's not having a problem, but how you deal with it. It's much better to seek help proactively rather than let the situation escalate and become a bigger problem.

If you're having difficulty in one of your groups or with one of your relationships, having other groups in your life is beneficial, as then the difficulty is just related to one aspect of your life rather than the whole of it (if you have just one group). This impacts less on your happiness, wellbeing and self-esteem. You also have support from the other groups to help you overcome any difficulty.

Broaden your perspective

It's only natural to feel overwhelmed from time to time. When you're facing something tough, it can feel enormous at the time. Like a deep dark hole, it's lonely and scary down there and you can worry you'll never get out. This is a typical response to finding something difficult. Remember, it's unlikely to be permanent and once you step outside of the hole, you can see things from a different angle. What additional perspectives might be helpful? What assumptions are you making? Sometimes talking to another person can help to do this. Refer back to the challenging thinking exercises and find an outlet to release the emotion you're experiencing. If things feel really difficult, refer back to Chapter 5 on unhealthy coping strategies and suicidal thoughts. Seek professional help.

Considering how you might feel once you've overcome this problem can be helpful. It helps you to understand the lesson you might be experiencing. You're also focusing on overcoming it which helps you to feel positive. You're acknowledging it's possible, it won't be forever and you're capable of overcoming this.

The resilience journey

Building resilience is an ongoing journey. Each time we experience difficulty or change, we learn things about ourselves. Each time you do, you might find it helpful to review the resilience evaluation at the beginning of this chapter (Exercise 22) and update your action plan. The more you build resilience, the more you build happiness. It also makes life easier and more enjoyable.

Guided Meditation 7: The Tree

Use this guided meditation to connect with your inner strength.

natalieread.online/tree

Summary

○ Life is full of ups and downs. Resilience helps us to cope with this and feel happier and supported on the journey in both personal and professional situations.

○ We need self-awareness and self-reflection to notice emotions, levels of stress, happiness and to be able to recognize the need for change or to overcome difficulties.

○ There's a difference between knowing about self-care and actually doing it. Investing in self-care helps you cope with life and builds happiness.

○ Knowing how to combat stress and create a nurturing environment is beneficial for your wellbeing.

○ Acknowledging and addressing problems as they arise prevents them from becoming bigger.

○ Having a good support network and being willing to ask for help when required is an important part of wellbeing and happiness.

○ Putting situations into perspective and challenging negative thoughts can help you to deal with the issue more quickly and effectively. Otherwise, it's easy to feel overwhelmed and become caught in a cycle of negative thinking.

Chapter 11

WRITING NEW
POSITIVE STORIES

'You're amazing, you're loved so much, you're really special, you're such a good friend, you're so valued, you contribute more than you know, we're so glad you're in the world.' How different would you feel, if you heard this every day? What difference would it make to your life? Imagine this as your internal dialogue. Imagine this type of encouragement coming from your teachers or employers? How differently would you feel? Just writing this, gives me a warm feeling. When I remember to say it to myself and to my children, it has a lovely impact. You may have doubts and reservations kicking in now. With a long time of saying something different, it's understandable. We need to work on believing this.

Hopefully, you now have a better awareness of your stories and their impact, as well as how they influence your perception, affect your self-esteem and are self-fulfilling. It's like re-reading the same story every day. It's not a problem if you're happy with your stories but unfortunately, this isn't always the case. Without realizing it, we can be caught in a story that we don't want. Have you ever watched a movie and guessed the ending? Life can be like this unless you're willing to make a change. What story would you like? We can't guarantee what happens in life but we can influence our interpretation and what we focus on. When we look for something positive, we can feel more positive. We create a positive cycle of momentum. Let's start now.

Gaining a new focus

What beliefs would you like to have in your life? What beliefs about yourself would make you feel happier and bring you peace? What difference would holding more empowering beliefs make to your life? These are important questions because they'll make you start to look for evidence that reinforces what you're focused on. It's the opposite process of how limiting beliefs become self-fulfilling. Instead, you're using the energy and focus to bring about positive change. You're changing your unique pair of glasses – upgrading them to notice positive evidence. You're feeding the Cherokee wolf a new diet of positivity and happiness. Like all new habits, this will require practice, energy and focus. You might have a few setbacks as you adjust but fundamentally, you're noticing a whole section of books you didn't think existed. Here's an example of how it can work.

I had a conversation with a six-year-old who came home from school feeling sad. She'd not been well the previous two days and was excited to be going back to school and seeing her friends. She described being disappointed about going back. She said her friends didn't seem to miss her. She felt sad all day and didn't really engage in playtime. She worried her friends didn't like her as much as another girl in her class. Her evidence for this was that the previous week, this girl had left school to go to a dentist appointment. When she returned, everyone was pleased to see her.

We discussed how upset she felt and how difficult it was to feel this way. We then discussed other possible interpretations of the story. She could see it was easier to miss a friend who'd been gone for an hour or so. They'd been playing a game in the morning before she left and she happened to come back just before afternoon playtime. Of course, they were pleased to see her to continue their game. From her scenario, being absent for two days wasn't noticed in the same way. There was no continuous game. She also returned to registration and lessons rather than playtime, so her friends were less able to show they'd missed her. By the time playtime came round, they'd probably forgotten she'd been away from school.

We discussed the analogy of stories. On the day that she returned to school, she could see she'd picked up a book with an unhappy ending. She'd formed the belief that she wasn't as important to her friends as the girl who went to the dentist. She spent the rest of the day collecting evidence so the story played out. She avoided her friends at playtime. She was quiet and spent time alone.

I asked her what story she'd like to have. She wanted to feel happy with her friends. We discussed what happy might look like. She identified she'd smile at her friends, join them at break time, laugh with them and suggest games they all loved to play. She decided to go to school with 'the happy book' in her bag. On the following day, she felt much happier. She had enjoyed playing with her friends and described a happy story. She had anticipated a happy story, looked for evidence to reinforce it and instigated situations to enable it. A simple example of how we can change our focus towards an ending we choose.

What's the evidence for positive stories?

As you can see above, we tend to spot what we look for and collect evidence that reinforces our belief whether it's positive or negative. Did you experience this for yourself in Chapter 3 by doing Exercise 5 on seeing the impact of your beliefs or by realizing how powerful beliefs can be through the example of Roger Bannister?

When I worked in the corporate world, I watched a video about Ben Zander, the conductor of the Boston Philharmonic Orchestra.[1] He discovered his students performed significantly better when they were given an A at the beginning of the year rather than the traditional method of gaining a result after your exams. By being told they had an A, I believe their confidence and belief in themselves was established from the outset. Rather than worrying about the result they might get, they were focused on maintaining their performance. This positive belief enabled them to 'act as if' they had already achieved it. By imagining achieving an A, you are believing in yourself and focusing on this as a possibility.

One of the general managers at the company where I worked believed that if you focused on measuring the result you desired, you were more likely to get it. Rather than the traditional sales targets, he created an additional goal of everyone breaking a record. Everybody had the autonomy to set their own records and any success was shared widely. Before long, records were being broken constantly. A culture of breaking records was established and it was one of the most successful years of company results. Much more effective than a pie in the sky sales target. People began to believe in themselves and, in many cases, achieved far more than they had ever anticipated. If you're focused on the change you want to see and you can believe it's possible, you're more likely to see it.

How positive affirmations can help

Positive affirmations are one of the easiest ways to make a change. An affirmation is a positive statement, such as 'I am happy'. You repeat the phrase at least 10 times, several times a day for a period of time and 21 days is recommended. It's important that the affirmation is positive and in the present tense. I've always found this a positive experience and felt better about myself for doing so. Now, there's scientific evidence to back it up. In one study by Falk and al,[2] it was discovered that saying health affirmations affected activity in a region of the brain and led to behaviour change. In another study by lead researcher Legault,[3] it was discovered that affirmations enhance performance and reduce anxiety, stress and defensiveness.

There was also some research by the Japanese scientist, Dr Emoto.[4] He examined water ice molecules under the microscope in response to words and music. With words such as 'love', the ice molecules appeared to have formed a beautiful structure. With words such as 'hate', the molecules appeared less so. I found this interesting given the amount of water we have within our bodies. What would our bodies look like with the usual internal dialogue? What difference could we make through kindness and self-compassion?

Exercise 25: Using affirmations

Try using affirmations for yourself. Firstly, identify an affirmation that you'd like to make. You could write your own or choose one from the list below. If you're writing your own, follow the same format: 'I am *[insert feeling or attribute]*' using the present tense and always stating a positive perspective. Some examples you might like to try:

- I am happy.
- I am healthy.
- I am likeable.
- I am lovable.
- I am OK.
- I am deserving of success.
- I am working to the best of my ability.
- I have good friends in my life.
- I have healthy relationships.

You can use your affirmation at any time during the day, but you might also like to try this process to help you fully absorb its meaning into your thoughts:

1. Find somewhere you feel relaxed and peaceful.
2. Imagine yourself as a tree with roots going into the ground through the layers of soil.
3. Sit or stand tall, imagining your back as the trunk of the tree. Imagine your head has branches stretching all the way to the sun. Place yourself in a golden bubble of protection.
4. Take some deep breaths letting go of anything that might get in the way of you receiving this.
5. Now focus on your heart area. Breathe in and out deeply from here. Imagine a connection with your heart as you say an affirmation that feels right for you at least 10 times. Notice how your heart feels – you should notice a warm feeling.

It's important that you say the affirmation with conviction. If you're wincing and full of doubt as you say it, it'll be ineffective. If this is the case, try something neutral for the first 21 days, such as 'I am OK.' and then move on to I am likeable and then I am lovable.

What gets in the way?

Our brains seem hardwired towards negativity. Research by John Cacioppo mentioned in an article by Marano showed a greater surge in electrical activity in the brain when exposed to negative stimuli.[5] This was thought to be related to our survival instincts because, in cavemen times, we needed a bigger reaction when facing a wild animal. You had to act quickly. Conversely, seeing a treat such as wild berries would be lovely but not a matter of life or death. You can take your time and enjoy the moment. So potentially positive images have a different impact. It's thought we need a ratio of five positive things to cancel out a negative image. So we need to work hard on positive stories and beliefs but it is possible.

Any new habit requires practice and perseverance. We also have defences that keep us in our old patterns. Remember the block in Chapter 7, the unhelpful coping strategies in Chapter 2 and the defences mentioned in Chapter 4? If you've worked on these and put into practice new behaviours, you'll start to notice progress. Let's move on to creating new stories.

Exercise 26: Creating positive stories

You might find it helpful to explore beliefs that are the opposite of the ones you currently hold. Or you could start with a clean sheet. You can follow the examples below or create your own.

For 'I'm likeable', write down:

* Everyone you've had a friendship with, even if you're no longer friends (we all have friendships that come to an end and all friendships have occasional disagreements). So include nursery, school and college friends, social groups, people you've met on holiday, at each workplace, in the community etc. Focus on all those happy, fun, meaningful, supportive, kind moments.
* Every family member you've had a good relationship with (even if you perceive you don't anymore). Remember that all relationships have their ups and downs and so we're not looking for perfection here.
* Every pet or animal you've felt a connection with.
* What your friends or family say about you that is likeable, e.g. kindness, humour.
* Something funny or quirky about yourself.
* What makes you unique, special or different from others.

- What enables you to work well with others, whether academically or in hobbies.
- Any other reasons you can think of.

For 'I'm a success', consider:

- Every exam (academic or non-academic) you've passed (don't dwell on those times when you could have done better – that's not the point!). Making steps towards this is also important to note so list the progress. Even if you failed, it's important to identify what you learned and how it helped you to improve.
- Every assignment you've handed in successfully (the definition of success is fit for purpose, not perfect).
- Everything you've been proud of in your life, e.g. charity fundraising, helping out friends, looking after animals, etc.
- Any new skills have you learned in your life, e.g. music, cooking, tennis, etc.
- What new situations you tried (whether they were successful or not, it doesn't matter, you tried) e.g. learning a new language, new foods, etc.
- What difficulties did you overcome? Think about moving schools and meeting new people, difficulties in friendships that led you to find new friendships,
- In which situations did you stand up for what you believe in? For example, a cause, standing up for somebody else, feeding back what was not OK about someone else's behaviour.
- What are you working on/improving on in yourself, no matter how small?
- What support have you given to others? This is anything that's helped somebody else academically, personally or in any other way.
- Any other reasons you can think of.

For, 'I'm attractive', consider the following:

- What physical characteristics do you like about yourself?
- What physical characteristics do other people comment on? (Consider from family, friends, as well as people you are attracted to.)
- What qualities or traits do you like about yourself?
- What qualities or traits do other people like about you?
- What qualities do you have that connect you to other people? For example, kindness, humour, being able to listen, taking an interest in others, being able to relax in other people's company, organizing events, etc.
- What's interesting about you? For example, what do you like, are interested in, what are you passionate about, what is quirky or different about you, what do you care about, what conversations do you feel most engaged in with others, what are your hobbies, etc?
- What are you passionate about? What gives your life meaning? Passion and believing in something are both interesting to others.
- How much do you like and appreciate yourself? Remember the more you're able to answer yes to this question, the more magnetic you are to others. It's also self-fulfilling.
- Anything else you can think of.

Once, you've identified the beliefs you'd like to focus on, try to add to your evidence on a daily or weekly basis. It might be strange at first but the more you do this, the easier it will become. Ask people you trust to help you build evidence while you get used to your new pair of glasses. Other people may already see you in this way and find it easy to help you. It's worth remembering that the more effort you put in, the more you'll benefit in the long run.

Let's go back to Simon from Chapter 3. Instead of looking at everything from the perspective of not being liked, he starts to consider all the evidence that he's indeed liked. He considers the evidence that he's invited to every social occasion, he has good conversations with Mark regularly, and he has a laugh with Joe and Mark frequently. Outside of the group, he realizes he's had more positive encounters with friends but he's been focusing on the one or two difficult times. Collecting evidence in this way helps him to see a more realistic picture. Doing this will either help you to feel better about yourself and your friendships or help you to see it may be time to find new friends.

Reframe your thoughts

Any time you find yourself slipping back into old habits, remember you're human. Thank the thought and recognize that it's trying to protect you in some way. Then try to reframe it. For example, instead of saying, 'I'm so rubbish at this', try telling yourself, 'I'm improving every day' or 'I'm working hard to improve.' Remember that using the present tense is important. If you're genuinely finding it difficult to think of anything positive, you might just be having an off day. Try again another day. Or revisit some of the previous chapters.

Exercise 27: Daily gratitude

There are many studies reporting on the benefits of gratitude to levels of stress, happiness, mental and physical health.[6] Here's a daily practice you can use to help bring more positivity and happiness into your life. It will help you to feel good about both yourself and life in general, and help to bring about a positive cycle.

1. Find somewhere relaxed and peaceful, then ground yourself by imagining yourself as a tree with roots going into the ground. Imagine your head has branches stretching up to the sun and place yourself in a golden bubble of protection.
2. Take some deep breaths focusing on your heart area.
3. From your heart, give thanks for everything you're grateful for. For example, you might say, 'I am grateful for the people in my life, my family who support me, the roof over my head, the sun, the beautiful tree in the garden, my health, the happiness in my life.' Be as specific as you can.
4. Each time you say thanks, feel your appreciation within your heart. Breathe it in throughout your whole body.

You could even try acknowledging the difficult situations you've overcome or are currently working through, strengthening a particular quality or moving on to a different path. This helps you see them from a different perspective, builds resilience and attracts positivity.

Critique yourself kindly

There's no such thing as perfect. Every human being has positive points and things they need to improve. As we explored in Chapter 7 on self-esteem, we all have an inner critic which, despite appearances, is actually trying to help us in life. It can be hugely beneficial to understand more about the intention of this critic and then try to model it on a more positive and nurturing voice. Another way to help this is to evaluate yourself from a positive perspective. Ask yourself:

•   What do I think I did well?
•   What do I think I could do differently or better next time?

We typically focus on what didn't go so well. By considering what you did well, you get used to noticing positive things about yourself. It takes practice but you'll find it becomes more comfortable over time. If you worry about boasting, think back to the A–Z continuum in Chapter 8. In my experience, people who think they might be boasting have nothing to worry about.

By asking yourself what you could do differently or better, you're immediately thinking about next time and focusing on moving forward. You're not stuck in negativity or something you can no longer do anything about. Instead, you're thinking about how to strengthen it further. Even if you require significant change, you're focused on how you can do it. See what difference it makes if you apply these questions to your presentations, written work or meetings.

Helping to build positive stories in others

In the same way that we're influenced by other people's actions, other people are influenced by what we say and do. Their reactions to events can be due to their stories. When we're faced with an accusation or misunderstanding, we'll naturally defend ourselves. Before we know it, we've been drawn into an escalating situation. If we can take a pause and try to correct the misunderstanding, we can prevent further issue.

For example, you might decide not to go to an event that you'd previously committed to. You're tired, a bit strapped for cash and in need of an early night. You communicate this to friends to let them know. You apologize for the change of plan. From your point of view, you don't like backing out of commitments and you don't do it very often. You're actually proud you're listening to yourself. You also do it knowing there are four other people going, so you're not really letting anyone down. In fact, it'll make it easier and cheaper for them in a taxi as five-seaters are rare in your area.

Unbeknown to you, two other people have also pulled out. This now leaves two people in the taxi which makes it more expensive for the others. Your friends are angry about being let down. It's been in the diary for a while and you've all been looking forward to it. They accuse you of conspiring with the others and not wanting to go in the first place. They're angry and it feels directed at you. It's understandable and human to be upset by this accusation. You might retaliate from a defensive place.

If you recognize your friend (who is a good friend) is reacting from a place of hurt and insecurity and you also recognise their story, you might be able to stay calm. They're not trying to hurt you but are responding in the moment. So we can help others with their negative stories by being more responsive and less reactive. We can also help build positive stories in others by giving positive feedback and showing them gratitude for their positive traits and behaviours.

Guided Meditation 8: The island
This guided meditation can help you clear any blocks and help you to create new happier, healthier stories in your life.

natalieread.online/island

Summary

- You can start to build positive stories by focusing on positive outcomes and looking for evidence to support them. Positive stories have a beneficial impact on self-esteem and happiness.

- ○ Developing a set of affirmations attuned to your situation and circumstances can also be helpful, especially when you use them daily over a 21-day period.
- ○ Developing a daily gratitude practice can help build a cycle of positivity.
- ○ Learn to critique yourself kindly and reframe the difficulties you face as opportunity areas that are more empowering and enable your ability to move forward.
- ○ Try to put yourself in the shoes of others and help them with their positive stories.

Chapter 12

A PATH
TO SELF-LOVE

If only you could see how special you are. You're a unique human being – there's no one exactly like you – even if you're a twin. You have your own talents, gifts, strengths and qualities that make you who you are. You also have annoying bits and things to learn. That's part of what makes you special. If you didn't have those, you wouldn't work on yourself and learn and grow. You wouldn't become who you're meant to be. It's easy to be sceptical about what I'm saying or to think you're an anomaly; much easier to think that, than acknowledge and appreciate just who you are. I urge you to explore what life could be like through a different lens. Even if you're not ready now, you might be one day. This chapter shows you how to follow a path of self-love.

How fear and judgement keep you small

You already know this path. How to be hard on yourself. How to judge. How to keep yourself small. To doubt yourself. Judgements perpetuate low self-esteem, low mood and anxiety. Underlying this path is an illusion of fear or lack – that we're somehow not good enough or flawed in some way. You can kid yourself that the path of self-love is about being big-headed or out of touch with reality but that's simply a defence mechanism that keeps you down (see also Chapter 8). We've already explored how scary it can feel to do otherwise and I understand where you're coming from.

Let's highlight the implications of this path through the analogy of an athlete. If you were a 110m hurdler, the path of fear is akin to creating additional hurdles to jump, in comparison to a usual race. It's much tougher than it needs to be. There's a greater propensity for injury and you use more energy than you need to. A whole season of races is a lot of hard work. The cumulative effort takes its toll. You use much more energy physically, mentally and emotionally. You may not even want to compete in the race and abandon it altogether. If those hurdles you're facing are assignments, projects, interviews, life challenges, how much harder is life for you? It's exhausting and demoralizing to even imagine it. No wonder you might feel low or worry. Let's look at an alternative path.

An alternative path of self-love

This path is about learning to accept who you are. Not striving to be a perfect human being. Not because you're in the right crowd. Not because you've achieved a particular thing. Not because you're in the football team. Not because you wear the right clothes. It's acceptance for who you are – a human being. Sometimes you won't like yourself. Some days you'll feel a bit low and feel like life's not working out. Perhaps you've said something you regret, you made a mistake or upset somebody. These flaws are not something to chastise. You're not horrible. You just made a mistake or are having a difficult phase. Everyone does. It's inevitable in life. You're still lovable. Instead of pushing these things away, you allow them to be. It's about unconditional love. Love without conditions. When we love and accept ourselves unconditionally, we accept our humanness – the amazing along with the mistakes. Sometimes it's the amazing qualities that are harder to own, by the way.

You're sending positive vibes to your hurdle race. You believe in yourself to do the best you can. It's not about being the best but giving it your best effort. Any setbacks along the way are helpful learning points rather than failures. By imagining that you can do it, you have the confidence to train. Any doubts along the way are information to improve your training. As you believe in yourself, you give yourself all the rest and nutrition you need. You have healthy coping strategies. Your body has the best chance of success. You believe in yourself but you're not attached to the outcome, otherwise, it becomes obsessive. Your positivity is motivational to you and others. You know if the race doesn't work out, it's something to learn from, for the next race. Or it might be a sign that you're in the wrong race. Maybe you'll find a new coach or team. Or you might even change sports – maybe you'll end up in the swimming team instead. If you're not feeling accepted by others (most of the time, not just a one-off), maybe your 'tribe' is elsewhere.

The benefits of self-love

When you have more self-love, you'll also have more confidence and self-esteem and feel more joy. You won't stop experiencing natural feelings in response to life events, but they're less likely to linger as you're less likely to add layers of judgement and resistance. You're more positive and trusting in life. Your health and wellbeing are enhanced as you're more likely to look after yourself. Sending positive vibes to yourself, your day ahead, your relationships and any important events is more effective than sending worry. Putting your energy and focus into something positive is much more enjoyable and life-enhancing than a cycle of worry or self-loathing.

When you have self-love, you don't allow anyone to disrespect you. It's less likely that you'll give yourself a hard time when you experience difficulties. You recognize you're lovable as you are. If a friendship or intimate relationship doesn't work out despite your best efforts, it wasn't right for you. You trust in the possibility there's someone else out there rather than fearing there's no one. When someone's feeling stressed and snaps at you, you recognize the situation for what it is. It's not because they're not nice or there's something wrong with you.

Thich Nhat Hahn, who is famous for his work on mindfulness, describes an exercise where you breathe in and out with your awareness focused on a particular part of your body.[1] As you breathe in, you acknowledge that part of your body and as you breathe out you set the intention to smile at this part of your body. You're effectively acknowledging and sending love to it. He describes how someone who focused this exercise on their lungs could no longer continue smoking. So imagine the impact of doing this regularly would have on you as a whole human being? You could do it by focusing on each body part, emotion or situation that you're drawn to.

Sources of unconditional love

You can practise sending unconditional love to yourself and situations by using the following process which you can adapt to suit your belief system. There are many different sources of unconditional love. Depending on your beliefs and preferences, you may have an affinity to one or other of the following. You might like to experiment with several before you decide the best choice for you. If you're used to self-criticism and worry, it can be hard to do this at first and like everything else, it takes time to build a new habit. The more you do this, the more beneficial and the easier it becomes.

- Imagining love from a higher perspective of yourself
- Love from your parents or carers
- Love from any person in the world
- Love from a religious figure or leader, e.g. God, Jesus, Mohammed, Krishna, the Dalai Lama, etc
- Love from a wise being, e.g. an angel, fairy, monk, etc
- Love from the sun
- Love from nature, e.g. the flowers, trees or animals, a special place, such as the beach or mountains
- Love from your experience of all your friends, relatives and people in the community collectively

Remember, unconditional love isn't dependent on you being a certain type of person or pleasing someone else; instead it's about just being as you are. Let go of any conflicts or differences as unconditional love goes beyond this.

Exercise 28: Sending unconditional love

There's a more extensive version of this exercise included at the end of this chapter (see Guided Meditation 9 – Unconditional Love). If it's safe and convenient to do so, you might choose to start by lighting a candle.

1. Ground yourself by imagining roots going from the bottom of your feet into the ground. Connect yourself to the sun by imagining you're a tree with branches coming from the top of your head and stretching out to the sun. Place yourself in a golden bubble of protection and affirm that you are 100 per cent safe and protected.
2. Imagine the source of unconditional love that resonates most with you from the above list.
3. See, sense and feel this coming into your body from above like a ray of sunshine. Imagine the colour, its qualities, the sound, resonance, what it feels like and anything else that makes it more real for you. (Not all of these questions

will resonate with you so just go with the ones that come naturally.) Spend a few moments noticing this and enjoying the feeling in your heart and body.

4. Imagine sending it to your emotions, thoughts and every part of your body. Send it to every part of your body from your heart. Send it to your day, including anything specific that's important to you, e.g. a relationship, piece of work or your health. Simply imagine the energy flowing all around these different aspects.

5. Acknowledge and thank any resistance that emerges and refocus on the exercise.

Spend as much time doing this exercise as you feel is appropriate. It should feel like an enjoyable experience that can be effective within only a few minutes; however, I encourage you to try this exercise daily for at least 21 days before judging its success.

You can also repeat the exercise at the end of the day and look back on your day; this can be particularly helpful if you have experienced any difficulties or feel stuck. You can even do this exercise during the middle of the day if you are experiencing something tough. It can help you to feel more positive about any situation.

Sending unconditional love to difficult situations/the past

You may find yourself dwelling on a conversation and wishing you hadn't said that. Why did your partner speak to you that way and what does it mean for your relationship? We all spend time analysing events from the past or imagining scenarios in the future from time to time. Sometimes, you're not even aware that you're doing it and before long several small events combine into something bigger. This can take a lot of time and lead you to feeling down about yourself, your life or even the world. If you want to feel differently, here's an alternative approach.

The next time you're faced with a difficult situation, acknowledge how you feel. Have compassion and love for all that's happened in the past to make you feel similar. For example, if you feel sad or angry, acknowledge the part of you that feels threatened, misunderstood or whatever else is triggering the sad and angry feelings. Acknowledge your humanness if you've made a mistake, said something you regret or wish you'd acted differently. Whether you're frustrated with yourself, someone else or a situation, visualize sending love to all those involved, including this part of you, to the past, to each person. In fact, anything connected to this situation can be beneficial. Repeat Exercise 28 above, but this time incorporate these elements.

When we send love and positive energy to difficult situations, we're acknowledging that everyone is human. We're not necessarily agreeing with all their actions or behaviours but willing to see the bigger picture. We don't know their intention behind the behaviour. It may seem as though someone is being unkind but this is our interpretation. Interpretations are based on our assumptions. Even if they're being unpleasant, what could that say about their story? By sending positive energy to the person, the situation will, at worst, stay the same and maybe even improve. Reflect on any action that you may wish to take from this place of love.

The more you do this, the more you're likely to feel the benefit. You may also like to send love to people who are experiencing difficulties, such as parts of the world that are suffering, to nature or any external aspect that you feel drawn to. Using Guided Meditation 6 – Loving Kindness (see Chapter 9) is another way to do this. I imagine that the more people who are able to do this, it will have a positive impact on the love and respect there is for this planet and lead to a reduction in the conflicts in the world. In fact, a study on meditation revealed that when a certain threshold of meditators was reached within a city, the level of crime there dropped between 1 and 7 per cent.[2]

Forgiveness

Forgiveness is an accompanying friend to this process. When you hold grudges and resentments, it's because you're holding onto feelings. Holding onto feelings adds them to the pan I described in Chapter 2 – the feelings that can be triggered at any moment. Do you feel better when you declutter your belongings? Imagine the impact on your life if you decluttered any old emotions and resentments? Debbie Shapiro describes how a lack of forgiveness keeps us in the role of victim. We stay locked in a relationship with the other person controlling our moods and emotions. The hurt is constantly recreated.[3] Forgiveness doesn't mean it was OK to treat you in that way or that what happened doesn't matter. It's about letting go of the feelings and energy that are involved in keeping the resentment. It releases the emotional intensity and any power that the other may still have over us. It's also about forgiving ourselves. We cannot accept ourselves fully if we don't accept everything about ourselves. It takes practice and can be difficult but the benefits are arguably worth it in the end.

Exercise 29: Forgiveness and letting go
Use this simple exercise to help you let go of past grudges and resentments and move forwards.

1. Ground yourself by imagining roots that lead your feet into the ground. Connect yourself to the sun by imagining

branches stretching from your head. Place yourself in a golden bubble of protection so that you feel safe.

2. Pay attention to your breath just as it is. Notice the journey of inhalation through your nose into your lungs and diaphragm. Then be aware of the journey of exhalation in reverse.

3. After a few breaths, bring your awareness to your heart. Breathe in and out from your heart.

4. Notice how this feels. Imagine love. Focus on what this both feels and looks like. The quality, colour, sound – whatever is relevant to you.

5. As you breathe in, acknowledge that you forgive yourself and imagine sending love on the out breath to yourself from your heart. You may feel emotion or recall memories from the past. Allow them to come and surround them with love from your heart. You may also need to release some emotion, so allow yourself to pause if you do. Keep sending love no matter what you're imagining. Remember unconditional love has no conditions.

6. Now repeat this for any person that may have wronged you in any way. Allow yourself any emotion. Remember, you're not necessarily condoning their actions but saying I am letting go of the burden of carrying this around. Imagine sending love from your heart to them, the situation and to yourself. If it's safe and convenient to do so, you might also like to light a candle for each person to affirm that you're forgiving and letting go.

7. When you feel this process is complete, blow out the candle. It might be that you have an insight about something that needs to be said. You can do this either in person or write it down on a piece of paper and then destroy it safely. You're not communicating in person but expressing something. Or it might be a lesson for yourself to consider.

You may need to repeat this exercise several times, as sometimes there are layers to different issues. You will probably notice feeling lighter after doing this exercise.

Sending unconditional love to the future

As well as difficulties in the present or the past, it's also beneficial to send unconditional love to situations in the future. You're worrying about an exam or interview. Scared of messing up a first date. Worried about how you're perceived by others. Concerned about how the future might be. It's understandable to worry but it can get you down. Worry can quickly escalate and affect your mood. Sending love to these situations is like acknowledging that you trust in yourself and life. You're sending positive vibes. It enables you to be more relaxed, in tune with yourself and be on the lookout for evidence of success. You zone out the negative noise in favour of your own intuition.

It doesn't have to be a situation you know about. It could be the future partner you've not yet met. The career path you've not yet decided on. The confidence you dream of. By sending love to these scenarios, you're allowing yourself to imagine it's possible and taking away hurdles that might be in the way. On the path of lack, worrying keeps you from starting the race. You're focusing on it not working out. Whereas on the path of self-love, your body language is poised for success, you're imagining it working out and easily spot opportunities that can help you with a positive outcome.

The future can also feel like something you're stuck with. You just can't see a way forwards. It feels like you are in an impasse. Sending unconditional love to this scenario helps you to acknowledge this is a temporary situation that will eventually pass. Every time you have a worrying thought, allow yourself to express the emotion and send love to help you overcome it. Repeat Exercise 28 above to send unconditional love to these future scenarios.

Catch your thoughts

When you judge yourself or have a worrying thought, acknowledge it. I imagine erasing it in a big flame being transmuted into something harmless – like love, peace or anything else that resonates. You can imagine a big eraser rubbing out your words or a brush or vacuum cleaning it up. Then reframe the thought into something positive and, again, repeat Exercise 28 by sending unconditional love to whichever scenario or impasse you're wanting to influence. Repeat over several days for the most impact.

Nonattachment

Remember not to create any expectation or attachments to the outcome. Doing so defeats the object of the exercise as it makes it conditional love. Sending love to your day or to a particular aspect of your life doesn't mean you'll only have happiness but it does mean a shift in perspective so it's easier to face anything. Going back to the hurdles, you pick yourself up from any fall. You know everyone has a fall from time to time. There's something to learn from the experience. This gives you the determination to continue. Even if you do go back to the old path of telling yourself off in the face of difficulty, you smile at the realization. Any berating of yourself is temporary. I use the analogy with clients of a spiral. The spiral continues to coil round and round in an upwards direction so although it may feel like you're revisiting the same place, it's from a slightly elevated perspective.

By sending love you're learning to accept where you are. I wish I knew about this when I struggled most with RSI. Sending love to this health issue would have helped me to accept what was happening more easily. The meditation would have helped me tune into myself and find solutions more quickly. Tending to a plant that's withering doesn't necessarily alter its fate but can improve its conditions and, you never know, the situation may alter positively after all.

Intention action outcome

In previous chapters we've explored how trying to control the outcome is usually futile. Instead, focusing on your intentions is more realistic and rewarding. I wanted to revisit this here as focusing on intentions also helps with strengthening self-love. If you focus on what you intend to happen and recognize this is coming from a good place, you're less likely to berate yourself. On the other hand, if you're wedded to an outcome you can never predict or control, it can lead to the illusion of fear and you may think, 'It didn't work out because I'm not good enough' – which is neither helpful nor true.

Criticism

Who do you hear most hear criticism from? Nobody particularly relishes hearing criticism but I imagine most people would say it's easier to hear it from people they know care about them. Someone who cares is less likely to make you feel bad intentionally. If you have self-love, you're more likely to have a kinder inner critic. You're more comfortable with yourself and so discern whether or not to take on another person's criticism. If you don't have self-love, the comment is likely to hurt as it reinforces what you already believe about yourself. When you have self-love, it doesn't hurt as much, as you recognize it may be a one-off, from somebody with a different perspective or something to learn from. You have more possibility. It's easier to hear feedback about how to hurdle with a different technique or approach.

Guided Meditation 9: Unconditional Love

Use this guided meditation to send love to yourself, others, the past and the future.

natalieread.online/love

Summary

- ○ Our experience of life is influenced by your choice of whether to believe in a perspective of unconditional love or not. Whatever your belief system, sending unconditional love to yourself, your relationships, life events, the past and the future can significantly improve how you feel. Just a few minutes each day can give you benefits.
- ○ Practising forgiveness and gratitude can be a positive experience.
- ○ It's easier to face criticism, grow from your experiences and carry out your day-to-day activities when you're on the path of self-love.
- ○ On the path of self-love, you can attract more positive scenarios and feel that life flows more smoothly.

Chapter 13

EMBRACING PEACE

You'll get the most from this chapter if you've worked on your stories (see Chapter 3) and understanding your anxiety (see Chapter 6). Hopefully, you'll then have a better understanding of your anxiety and how to manage any symptoms healthily. You'll also understand how your stories compound your anxiety.

In this chapter, we'll explore a completely different approach to working with anxiety and fear. Instead of focusing on what we don't want, we're going to focus on what we do. We'll build on the principles behind writing a new story or navigating a path of self-love, but this time focused on bringing about more peace in your life. We'll also incorporate some of the principles of mindfulness into the picture. It's easier to accept and enjoy being human when we're more present with ourselves and have more compassion and less judgement.[1]

The present moment

What did I say that for? Why did that have to happen? What if I can't get hold of that book tomorrow? What happens if I fail? We all tend to dwell on things from time to time, on what's already happened or might happen in the future. Who's not ruminated over a conversation wishing that you'd said something else, or not at all. We also have times when we agonize over possible future scenarios, no matter how far-fetched they are. It can be exhausting considering different scenarios and can lead to anxiety, low mood and low self-esteem. The process can also be futile as the past cannot be changed and the future has many possibilities, not certainties.

It can be helpful to learn from the past – what's behind my low marks or what stories feed into my self-esteem? It's also a good idea to prepare for the future – what do I need to do to make my year abroad successful? Yet, too much evaluation or preparation can be detrimental to happiness. How much more would you enjoy life if you savoured every moment? Enjoyed conversations without analysing what you've said. Danced without scrutinizing your every move. Enjoyed a walk without processing your to-do list. You'd be able to connect with yourself and others more fully. Have more energy as you're focused on fewer things. Your inner critic would be less dominant. You'd notice beautiful things in nature and in others. You'd be less likely to respond on automatic mode. Life would be less like a treadmill and you'd have more joy and less anxiety.

Take Justin, for example. One day Justin wakes up feeling low. He carries out his usual routine and goes off to work. The low feeling lingers around but he's able to work throughout the morning. At lunchtime, he's in his regular cafe at the usual time but can't see any of the friends he normally sits with. He was hoping to see them as he's got a presentation this afternoon that he's dreading. He's mentioned it to a few of them and is disappointed they didn't remember. He's going over and over scenarios about the presentation. Picturing it not going well. He's also ruminating over yesterday's conversation about meeting up for lunch. Why did his friends let him down? They knew how important it was for him to meet up. He goes back to his desk and can't do any work. He's caught in a spiral of negative thoughts. Do his friends really care about him? What if he makes a fool of himself this afternoon? Is he cut out for this job? His low mood has become worse. He's feeling really anxious to the point that he's nauseous and shaking and doesn't know how he's going to deliver his presentation this afternoon.

Justin decides to take a walk. He recognizes he's in a cycle of negative thinking based on some old stories. He knows he fears failure and being unlikeable. He's worked on these stories before and spots the signs. He recognizes the patterns and knows if he doesn't do something about it, the thoughts and feelings will continue to escalate. He understands his anxiety and knows when it's heightened, he's afraid he'll fail or be rejected. It's helping him to avoid these fears being realized but it needs more work to be effective in doing so. He also knows it's easy for the thoughts and feelings to escalate and become self-fulfilling. He takes a walk around the garden and concentrates on breathing deeper (see Exercise 9 on deep breathing in Chapter 6). By noticing his surroundings in the garden and being focused on his breathing, this enables him to be more present and he immediately feels a little calmer. He also practises a body awareness scan as he knows this can be helpful.

At the end of this chapter, you'll find Guided Meditation 10, Body Awareness Scan, which you can use to help you recognize your physical sensations, emotions and thoughts. During this meditation, you scan your body from head to toe from the place of a compassionate observer. You're not judging why or how long something will be there. Instead, you're describing what you notice without any judgement. For instance, 'There's a feeling in my heart area... it feels sad... empty... like a black hole... it spreads from my heart up to my throat.' You don't have to make sense of the feeling or sensation but by acknowledging it, you're affirming it. It doesn't need to vie for your attention anymore. By not judging, you're allowing it to be. You're not adding any additional layers of judgement or resistance. It may be able to move on by itself or you might recognize some action you wish to take. By focusing on the present moment, you escape the racing thoughts and feelings. Practising this scan regularly will bring the most benefit.

Thoughts, feelings and sensations are not fixed

The more you practise the body awareness scan, the more you notice that thoughts, feelings and body sensations are not fixed. They come and go. What you feel in one instance, is not necessarily how you'll feel later. You might feel angry right now but later on, you feel happy. This is true for any feeling, thought or bodily sensation. While thoughts have patterns, they vary depending on how we're feeling on a particular day. It's when we fear we're stuck with something, such as low mood, feeling hopeless or feeling pain,that it's harder to cope with as you start resisting them. By realizing that thoughts, feelings and sensations come and go, they're easier to bear. You can detach from them. If you're having a bad day or feeling sad, accepting it's natural and will pass, it helps the thought or feeling to dissipate by itself.

After doing the body awareness scan, Justin notices he's feeling sad, stressed and anxious. His muscles are tense and he has a sick feeling in his stomach. His thoughts are about fear of failure, getting the presentation wrong and whether his friends like him. Although he'd identified these thoughts before the body awareness scan, he feels differently now. It's enabled him to acknowledge these thoughts and take a step back. He recognizes his thoughts are loaded with assumptions and influenced by his stories. He can acknowledge his fear. The body awareness scan helps him focus on what he's experiencing in the present moment. He can breathe into this. Deep breaths in and out. Breathing helps to take the focus away from his thoughts and also helps him to feel calmer as it reduces the stress hormones in the body. He can acknowledge his humanness. He knows that his thoughts and feelings come and go and although this feels like the truth in this moment, it may not be *the* truth. He knows that he experiences feeling differently at other times.

Self-compassion

It's easy to judge yourself. To focus on what you're not doing or should be doing. Self-compassion requires patience, practice and intent. You might remember from earlier chapters that judgment and fear add layers to the original feeling. Just because you feel angry now doesn't mean you're an angry person. You're a human being who's feeling angry at that particular moment. The more we can learn to understand our emotions and know they're part of being human, the easier this process will be. Judgement is typically connected to fear of the unknown or of the past repeating itself. Being self-compassionate helps you to acknowledge you're a human being doing your best and sometimes life is challenging.

Justin acknowledges it's natural to feel anxious and doubt yourself before a presentation. He doesn't berate himself for feeling like this. He can see it's compounded by his stories from the past. By recognizing this, he can feel self-compassion for the hurt he's experienced. It's understandable he's felt that way and that he's tried to avoid experiencing the same again. He recognizes his story is based on his interpretation of the situation at the time. He realizes there are other interpretations to his conclusion that he was a failure and unlikeable. He identifies his anxiety can become heightened when he fears being hurt or failing again. By acknowledging this, he's able to reframe the situation.

Reframing in action

He tells himself, 'It's natural to feel anxious before a presentation. This job's important to me. I've prepared as much as I possibly can and I deserve to do well. If anything goes wrong, there's something to learn but it's probably not as bad as I'm imagining. I'm experiencing intense low mood and anxiety because it's triggered the memory of my past hurts. This was a difficult time and my reaction to these was understandable. My heightened anxiety is trying to help me do well. I have no idea about what happened at lunchtime but I can let that go until after the presentation. I'm making assumptions based on my old stories. These stories are in the past.' Justin still feels anxious but it's much more manageable. He's able to carry on with the presentation. He's feeling better about himself. When he next sees his friends, he's also in a better place to have a conversation with them rather than in the midst of his stories and anxiety. He can respond from a more reflective place rather than on autopilot.

Savouring the moment

It's not just about dealing with anxiety, low mood or difficult events. Learning to be more present and self-compassionate, also allows you more peace and joy. Being able to notice your senses – what you can see, hear, feel, smell, taste – you'll notice there are wonders to be had from savouring every mouthful of food, experiencing the water on your skin while showering, walking to any destination and everyday routine tasks purely by being mindful in the moment. Not only would you enjoy more of these things but arguably you'd be healthier also. Chewing your food and eating more slowly enables digestion. If you're consciously walking or running, you're less likely to trip or run into something. It's natural to be distracted in the process, so just acknowledge your distracting thoughts and refocus on your senses. The more you do this, the easier it becomes.

While working, playing sport or participating in hobbies, being more focused on the present helps productivity and performance as you're focused on the task in hand rather than listening to your internal dialogue. For example, if you're writing something and constantly telling yourself you're rubbish, you can't do it and everybody else is better, it's hard to produce a good piece of work. It's also likely to take you much longer and cause much angst. It's also helpful to dis-identify from the critic by breathing in self-compassion and unconditional love, as we did in the previous chapter.

Exercise 30: Performance – sports and hobbies[2]

While playing your favourite sport, doing exercise or hobby focus completely on the task in hand. So if, for example, you're playing a racquet sport, notice the position of your feet, where the ball hits the racquet, the position that you're hitting the ball, e.g. in front, waist high. Make any adjustments you think would be most helpful, e.g. hitting the ball in the top middle of the racquet (the sweet spot).

You might decide a different focus, such as the position of your feet or a place in the court, you're aiming for. Determine your point of reference and remain focused on this aspect alone without spilling into judgement. It's about curiosity and presence.

The contrast to how you usually play is that you're not focusing on comments such as, 'I'm rubbish, my opponent is better than me, that was crap and so on.' All of these thoughts lead to low confidence and frustration and will also affect your performance negatively. Negative thoughts and feelings are natural and understandable but instead of believing them, you acknowledge them as thoughts rather than the truth. You keep returning your focus to your point of reference. The more you do this, the easier it will be.

If you feel it's hard to shake off self-criticism, take a few moments to ground yourself by imagining roots going into the ground from your feet, connecting yourself to the sun by imagining branches stretching up from your head and imagining a golden bubble surrounding you keeping you safe. Imagine your source of unconditional love (as in Exercise 28 in Chapter 12) coming down through the top of your head and filling your body. You can also send it to the task in hand by visualising the unconditional love surrounding it. See, sense and feel this positive energy and enjoy the experience. Do this for a few minutes until you feel differently.

Try refocusing on your sport or hobby or decide to leave it for another day. Typically, you will find it easier to focus after doing this.

It's not about stopping thoughts or feelings but instead choosing how much attention to give to them. It helps to acknowledge them by saying, 'Thank you, I know it's meant to be helpful but I am focusing on [*insert what you're focusing on*].' After the practice, you might evaluate how it's gone and make changes.

Exercise 31: Performance – writing and creating

While writing or creating, focus on how your hand feels as you hold the pen or come into contact with the keyboard. Your body posture, the pen coming into contact with the paper. How many sources you're using, the amount of writing you're doing. You might want to keep writing until you reach a certain section of the page without judging anything.

Of course, you'll be inundated with thoughts, physical sensations and feelings while completing the task, and know this is to be completely expected. While you might not like a particular thought or feeling, know that it's natural to have thoughts and feelings and that it's understandable not to like them all. As a thought or feeling arises, acknowledge it and let it pass without becoming attached to it being true. Avoid getting into a dialogue of what it might mean and how long it will be there by thanking it and returning to your focus point.

Keep focused on the task in hand. If your thoughts or feelings get particularly loud, it might be an indication that you need a break. Try some breathing, take a walk or take a longer break. If you feel it hard to shake off self-criticism, take a few moments to ground yourself by imagining roots into the ground from your feet, connecting yourself to the sun by imagining branches stretching up from your head and imagining a golden bubble surrounding you and keeping you safe. Imagine your source of unconditional love (as in Exercise 28 in Chapter 12) coming down through the top of your head and filling your body and the task in hand. See, sense and feel this positive energy and enjoy the experience. Do this for a few minutes until you feel differently. After doing this, try to refocus on your work or take a break.

There is, of course, a time to engage the inner critic in terms of evaluating whether the piece of work is good enough. Determine when the best time to allow this and set a limit so that it does its job but without hijacking the project. The goal is to allow yourself to improve what you've written. Hopefully, using unconditional love helps your critic to become more self-compassionate over time. If you do feel stuck, you potentially need more clarity on what will help you move forwards. Seek an additional perspective or take some time out. As time goes on, you'll hopefully be able to more finely tune your critic to reality so that it's a helpful barometer when you need it.

When you focus on anxiety

Like James in Chapter 2 or Mary in Chapter 5, when we don't like something we tend to want to stop it. We just want to feel better and, ideally, in the easiest way possible. We focus on getting rid of the symptoms. It's natural but it doesn't always have the outcome you desire. The more you push away your anxious thoughts, the more overwhelmed you can feel. You'll probably worry whether or not you'll get better. When? How? It's hard to think positively from this frame of reference. Thoughts spiral into negative thinking cycles. You notice your body's not coping physically. Your mood deteriorates. You're overwhelmed on all fronts. You try to tackle this with more focus on stopping the symptoms. The cycle continues.

To see how powerful this is, just imagine you're about to sit an exam or go into an interview; that your friends don't really like you or tomorrow's going to be a bad day. You're probably thinking I know that's not real, so you're not really worried. Yet, I'm guessing you're not as comfortable as before I mentioned it. The mind is so powerful that imagining any negative scenario can create negative feelings. Watching scary films can bring about nightmares as you struggle to differentiate between imagination and reality. Remember how powerful your stories are – regardless of how true, you believe them.

You get what you focus on

Apparently, it's statistically more likely that a child will drop something if told, 'Don't drop that' than if you say, 'Hold on tight.' You can see this for yourself by imagining the following: tell yourself not to think about elephants, only tigers. Just in the process of saying elephant, an image of an elephant is likely to form in your mind. It would be more effective to just give the positive instruction by saying, 'Imagine a tiger'. We can't really test this theory using the same example, as you're likely to still have the image of both of them. So this time my instruction is to focus on a beautiful sunny day. Imagine you have a lovely clear image now, without confusing it with the image of a rainy day. I watched a documentary years ago about sports psychology. The English football (soccer) squad improved their penalty shootout rate when they focused on imagining the ball going into the net. This was more effective than worrying about failure.

We discussed the benefits of focusing on the change you wanted to see in Chapter 11. This is equally true with anxiety. If you've worked on your anxiety – you're aware of how it's trying to help, what helps it and what makes it worse. A different approach may help you to find a new level of peace – by focusing on gaining peace rather than ridding yourself of anxiety. In the same way that focusing on a negative scenario creates negative feelings, imagining a positive scenario can generate positive feelings. The more positive your beliefs, the more positive evidence you're likely to collect.

Catch your thoughts

The more aware you are of your thoughts, the more you can check whether you're focusing on positive or negative scenarios. As thoughts are often automatic and subconscious, this takes practice. You'll inevitably have a negative thought from time to time so it's not about being perfect. Each time you catch yourself with one that's limiting, acknowledge it. You might want to do some work on yourself such as work on your story or let go of some emotion. After acknowledging the thought, you can imagine cancelling it out. Like an eraser on a piece of paper or the delete button on your computer screen. You could even imagine vacuuming it up or sweeping it away or it vanishing into a flame. Whatever works for you. Once you've acknowledged and let go of the thought, identify what quality you'd like instead.

Why focus on a quality?

Focusing on a quality is more effective than imagining an outcome. Rather than fixating on a particular partner, friendship group or specific outcome, focus instead on the quality you'll feel. If you focus on happiness or peace, it's a much more relaxing experience. It helps you let go of the anxiety. Conversely, focusing on an outcome creates tension, expectation and possibly more anxiety. You're attached to the result. You're trying to control rather than going with the flow of life. If you're focused on a quality, you open up more possibilities and opportunities. Maybe there's another partner, friend, career path that's more suitable than the one you have in mind. It will be harder to find these if you've determined the outcome already. Here are some examples of qualities:

Worrying thought/emotion	Alternative positive quality to focus on
Fear or anxiety	• Peace • Calm • Tranquillity
Rejection	• Acceptance • Peace • Love
Failure	• Happiness • Trust • Success
Things going wrong	• Joy • Peace • Trust

The more you do this, the easier it'll become. Each time you doubt the process, remember the impact you can have on your wellbeing from focusing on more positive scenarios. If you're not sure what quality to go for, peace is a good option. When you have peace, you naturally have other qualities as well. By not attaching to the outcome, you're fostering trust.

This helps us to go with the flow of life and in doing so, makes life more flexible, opens up opportunities and helps us to enjoy the journey. Here's a process to do this.

Exercise 32: Turning worry into a positive scenario
You recognize you're worrying about something, e.g. negative thoughts or emotion and you recognize the signs of anxiety physically. Acknowledge to yourself you're feeling anxious and that this is being made worse by the spiralling thoughts.

1. Write down any thoughts that are going round your mind. This is to 'park them' so they are acknowledged. Revisit Exercise 11 on helping anxiety to do its job in Chapter 6, if appropriate, to identify any action that might be helpful. It's important to listen to the underlying message within the feeling.
2. Remind yourself that thoughts aren't necessarily the truth. There are inherent assumptions. It's more productive to focus on a positive scenario. Use whichever image resonates with you to clear away the negative thought, e.g. vacuum cleaner, flame, delete button, eraser, etc.
3. Acknowledge to yourself that it's more effective to focus on what you want rather than dwell on what you want to get rid of. Remember all of the times you've experienced feeling peace in the past. The more memories you can think of will help remind you of how possible this is. Remind yourself how peace feels. What do you notice in your body when you're experiencing peace?
4. Now turn to the end of this chapter and use Guided Meditation 11, Focusing on Positive Qualities.

You might like to light a candle dedicating it to your intention, remembering not to attach to the specific way that this will come about. If any doubting thoughts or judgements arise, acknowledge them and then continue to focus on the exercise. If it's difficult for you to trust this will work out, it's highlighting there may be something to work on or it's a habit. It may be helpful to revisit Exercise 20 on working with the block in Chapter 7.

Imagine Zoe who's just moved into a house. All her roommates are out for the day and she's glad of the peace and quiet. She's inundated with work and can finally make some headway. Halfway through the morning, water starts running down the walls. It's torrential rain outside and she realizes there's a leak. The roof's not long been done and so she tries to contact the landlord. His phone diverts to voicemail. She can't reach her roommates. She does what she can in the attic, putting buckets out to catch the drips. It's still not enough. She starts to worry about what she'll do if she doesn't get hold of the landlord. Would the landlord expect her to contact a roofer? She then thinks about how wet and damp the house will be. How much will it affect them? She's now spent over an hour dealing with this and how much longer will it take? She's now not going to get done what she had planned. Her mind's racing with what ifs.

Zoe recognizes she's in a negative cycle which will continue until she makes an intervention. She follows the steps in the exercise above, reminding herself that she's doing the best she can in an unfortunate scenario. She reminds herself that her imagined scenarios are not necessarily true. She imagines a vacuum clearing away the negative cycle of thoughts. She visualizes feeling calm and at peace during the meditation. She feels much better and more trusting that everything will work out. She lets go of trying to solve the issue and starts to focus again on her work with this more positive mindset. She recognizes she can do no more than she's done already. Interestingly, 10 minutes after listening to the meditation, her landlord calls and thanks her for what she's done so far. He takes the whole situation off her hands and she is able to do a whole afternoon of productive work.

Nurturing environments

To enhance your feeling of peace, it's worth paying attention to your environment. Limiting exposure to bad news, violent TV, social media and anything else that gives you fear or a sense of comparison to others. Walk frequently in nature, spend time with kind and caring people, allow time for relaxation and fun, practice positive thinking and having good self-care. These can all help you to feel more at peace in your life.

Guided Meditation 10: Body Awareness Scan
Use this guided meditation to become more aware of your physical sensations, thoughts and feelings from the place of a compassionate observer.

natalieread.online/scan

Guided Meditation 11: Focusing on Positive Qualities
Use this guided meditation to help yourself focus on what you want rather than what you don't.

natalieread.online/focus

Summary

○   You can increase your happiness by detaching from past and future scenarios and savouring more of the present moment with more self-compassion and less judgement. Spending time in the present moment is called 'mindfulness.'
○   Using Guided Meditation 10, Body Awareness Scan can help you see that physical sensations, emotions and

thoughts come and go. They don't define who you are as a person and if you don't judge them, they pass more quickly.

○ You can improve your performance, productivity and confidence by detaching from the inner critic and focusing on the task in hand.

○ Focusing on what you would like to come about, without attaching any outcome to it, is a much more productive strategy than fearing what you don't want. It also helps to increase the chance of it happening and feels more positive. Focusing on qualities is more effective than focusing on a specific outcome.

○ The 12 guided meditations (see Appendix I) and being conscious of your breath (as in Exercise 9 on deep breathing in Chapter 6) can also help to bring you a sense of peace and help you feel more confident about managing difficulties.

Chapter 14

STRENGTHENING IDENTITY AND BALANCE

We all go through a separation process from our parents or carers and become individual human beings in our own right – it's a natural and essential process to forming our own sense of who we are. You may hear people talk about needing to 'go find themselves'. Sometimes people believe they're clear on their identity but something then happens to refine this. Without a clear understanding of your own identity: wishes, needs, decisions, subconsciously, you may be trying to please others or trying to conform to expectations. When you're saying yes to something, you're saying no to something else. If you're following a path in conflict with your own desires and wishes, it can lead to depression. Given this impact, it can be helpful to make this process conscious.

Essentially, you're trying to make sense of all the things you might take for granted, for example:

- Do I love hockey because I love hockey, or because I thought I had to play it?
- Did I become a tomboy because I wanted to be a tomboy, or did I feel pressured to be like my friends?

- What do I actually like wearing?
- What do I like doing?
- Am I comfortable with my sexuality?
- What beliefs and values are important to me?
- Do I consciously know how these influence me?
- How do I measure myself and does this help or hinder me?
- What career do I really want?
- What makes me happy?
- What brings me peace?
- What am I passionate about?
- Do I spend time on activities and with people that enable this?

It's OK not to know the answers to these questions. It takes time to explore and answer them. Sometimes you'll need to do the things that aren't right for you in order to know what is. It's about taking steps towards finding out. Hopefully this chapter will help you in this process.

The benefits of a strong sense of self

We explored in Chapter 7, the importance of measuring ourselves from an internal focus. It's such an important point that I wanted to revisit it here. It's natural to want to please others, receive positive comments, get likes on social media and to want to do well in life – but if you don't have a strong sense of self, not receiving them can be devastating. The more you feel comfortable with who you are, the more you can put this into perspective. Exercise 18 on looking for positives in Chapter 7 is a way to help you focus on more empowering measures.

When you know more about who you are, you can allocate time to do the things that you want to do. Refer back to Exercise 2 on what's important and brings you happiness in Chapter 1 and make decisions in line with this. You know the kind of people you want to spend time with and how to pick yourself up when you're feeling low. You're comfortable spending time in your own company. You know when you're out of balance or in need of a change. You have a sense of the contribution you'd like to make in your lifetime. When you have this level of connection and self-understanding, you'll discover there's more health, balance, happiness, self-acceptance and peace in your life.

What do you value?

If you know the values that are most important to you, life can be easier. It helps you to identify people or situations that will be compatible, allocate how you spend your time and identify your triggers. If one of these values is not being met, you're likely to be feeling upset or angry. Knowing your values helps you to make decisions and identify what might be missing from your life. You'll also feel better about yourself the more you live by your own values. Here's a list of values although it's not an exhaustive list. You may notice some additional ones that are important to you.

- Integrity
- Trust
- Security
- Freedom
- Growth
- Love
- Respect
- Nurture
- Equality
- Fairness
- Openness

- Authenticity
- Health
- Honesty
- Positivity
- Generosity
- Kindness
- Non-discrimination
- Learning
- Support
- Fun
- Joy
- Happiness

Exercise 33: Your values

Write down the values that are important to you. Consider which ones are being fulfilled and which ones you could meet further. For example, fun and freedom are important to you but you realize you don't spend enough time on activities that fulfil this need.

Identifying your 'parts'

We've already discussed the concept of parts and explored the inner critic and anxious subpersonalities in previous chapters but you can identify other subpersonalities in addition to these. For example, you may have a part of you that works really hard, a part that wants to rest, a part that wants to party all day, a part that wants to save the world, an activist, a pleaser and so on. Through recognition of these different parts, you might recognize which ones are dominant (which you identify most with) and the ones you are least familiar with. This awareness allows you the opportunity of more harmony. For example, you may notice the part of you that wants to work really hard is most dominant but the part of you that needs rest or time for fun is often ignored. If you continue ignoring these parts, they may sabotage your day at some point in order to get their needs met. Through awareness, rather than this happening subconsciously on an inconvenient day, you can manage a conscious way to meet their needs that better suits you.

Exercise 34: Understanding your parts[1]
Identify your different parts or subpersonalities, e.g. critic, inner child, driver, self-care, athlete, couch potato, pleaser, environmentalist, etc. You can also do this exercise by identifying the different roles you have in life or your different character traits.

1. Write or draw the different parts on a piece of paper. You might like to build a character/image for each one.
2. Once you have identified each of your parts, consider the advantages and disadvantages of each one.

    • Which ones are the most dominant?
    • Which ones do you least identify with?
    • What are their needs?
    • Are their needs being met?
    • What could bring about more harmony?

The self-compassionate mediator

It's helpful to be aware of your own self-compassionate mediator[2] who can help bring in line the different subpersonalities. A self-compassionate mediator is a bit like your internal CEO making decisions about which projects to be involved in and who's best to do so. When I was training in psychosynthesis, we talked about the conductor of the orchestra helping each of the individual instruments (subpersonalities) to play a harmonious tune, rather than all of the instruments playing out their own agendas with disregard to the overall tune. It's important that the mediator is calm, wise and decisive in a respectful way while also being able to understand the overall picture and the direction you're headed. The mediator needs to be self-compassionate and objective to do its job.

The self-compassionate mediator helps you to make decisions, take rest when you need to, identify projects and hobbies to be involved in and whose company you'd most benefit from spending time with. When you're in contact with this part of you, you're happier, more confident and self-assured and also have a stronger sense of self. You know you're in contact with the self-compassionate mediator when you feel self-compassionate, love and wisdom about yourself and decisions. If you feel self-criticism or any other less positive emotion, you're more likely to be in touch with your critic or other dominant subpersonality. If this is the case, congratulate yourself on noticing this as awareness is an important precursor of change. The following activities can help you strengthen your connection with your self-compassionate mediator:

- Practice regularly Guided Meditation 10, Body Awareness Scan, in Chapter 13 and reflect on the self-compassionate observer.
- Practice Guided Meditation 9, Unconditional Love, and Exercise 28 to bring in unconditional love in Chapter 12 to help you connect with a more self-compassionate place.
- Spend time in nature (see Exercise 35 below).
- Spend more time doing activities where you feel 'in the zone', free from judgement and thought. For example, dancing, painting, time in nature, etc.
- Spend more time in meditation and self-reflection.

It takes time and effort to do this so allow yourself lots of patience, time and opportunity to do so.

Exercise 35: Walking in nature

This exercise is especially effective if you're feeling stressed, overwhelmed with emotion or feeling that life is not quite working out. Go to somewhere in nature where you like to be and feels safe. Give yourself a good 20 minutes or more, if possible. You can do this exercise walking or by sitting somewhere comfortable.

Walk briskly trying to imagine grounding yourself as you do so – visualize roots coming out of your feet and going into the ground beneath you. Connect to the sun by imagining branches stretching from your head and place yourself in a golden bubble of protection.

Observe your breath for a while and then try to breathe a little more deeply. On the in breath, give yourself permission to relax and enjoy the time you have allocated. On the out breath, imagine releasing all of the tension and worries from your body.

Focus your senses for at least a few minutes, or as long as you can or would like to, on your surroundings. Notice what you can see – the colours, shapes in the clouds, wildlife big and small, the details in the leaves, and so on.

Then turn your attention to what you can hear – the wind, the sounds of nature, distant traffic, your footsteps, and so on.

Then focus on your physical sensations, such as your feet coming into contact with the ground, the wind or sun on your face, your breath, your clothing coming into contact with your skin, the movement of your body as you walk, and so on.

Then you might like to walk along without focusing on anything. Allow thoughts to come and go as they please without getting caught in rumination or analysis. You're likely to feel calmer by stepping out of your thoughts. You may even find you have a different perspective than before the walk.

If after doing this, you still fill in need of a boost of positivity, use Exercise 28 on sending unconditional love in Chapter 12.

Balance

It's one thing knowing what's important to you and another thing to actually put it into practice. You need to consciously evaluate how you spend your time and the impact of this. Below is an exercise that can help.

Exercise 36: Life-balance audit

How would you rate the following areas – note that some may be irrelevant or unimportant to you and you may need to add additional areas, such as working in the community. For each one of the areas rate it from 1–10 the following:

* Importance: Rate it from 1–10, where 1 is not important at all and 10 is vitally important.
* Current time (quantity and quality): Rate it from 1–10, where 1 is not at all and 10 is many hours.
* What action is required to bring this into balance/increase happiness?
* It may be helpful to reflect on Exercise 34 understanding your parts and make sure you have included all aspects of your subpersonalities.

Hobbies and interests

Involved in a variety of activities:

* Include things you enjoy, are good at and feel you are progressing in. Also, ones you enjoy doing with people you like spending time with.

Health

* Physical health (good nutrition, drinking plenty of water, regular exercise – aerobic, flexibility and strength building, good quality of sleep etc.)

- Emotional health (awareness, acknowledgement and expression versus repression, doing things that make you feel happy, having fun, taking responsibility for life as opposed to having a victim mentality etc)
- Mental health (being mindful about thoughts, activities that relax and destress you, actively working on your journey, activities that help with focus, memory and concentration)
- Spiritual health (prayer, chanting, meditation, yoga, reading, time in nature, gratitude, reflection time to work on self, finding inner peace and acceptance of self and others)

Family and friends
- Partner
- Wider family
- Friends and general social life

Career/job
- Current studies/job
- Future job or aspirations/building resume

Meaning

Time for your passions, beliefs, causes, helping others, community, time on your own, etc.

Bringing life into balance

Do you need more balance or happiness in your life? If you imagine a table with glass bottles on it, each glass bottle represents one of your headings above, e.g. health, career, etc. We're all different, so on your unique table you'll have the unique amount of bottles that fits comfortably for you. Imagine that each bottle is filled with an amount of liquid that helps it to stay balanced on top of the table. The whole table is balanced when each bottle is filled appropriately. So balance is achieved when you are spending the appropriate amount of time with each important activity in your life. If you spend too much or too little time on one bottle, it will not only affects that bottle but also could knock over the other bottles as it loses balance. Which of your bottles needs attention? If you ignore a niggling relationship or an emerging issue at work, they'll only get worse.

Some people find it helpful to apportion time to ensure they have balance in life. It doesn't have to be prescriptive – it's more about what feels right. Whichever way you create balance, try to have flexibility. You might need to take a break or do some exercise if you're feeling overwhelmed. Also be prepared to make changes. If you have an important deadline, you might need to reduce other activities temporarily and increase your self-care.

Setting goals

Another way to consider balance and happiness, is to take a long-term review of your life. In the next week, month, year, five years, what do you want to achieve? Consider this from all of the perspectives of the life-balance audit. If you're feeling stale, identifying two things to do each week, month, year and so on, helps you to feel you're going in the right direction. For example, visiting a new place or intending to try something new on a menu might be in a weekly or monthly goal. This stops you going from week to week without doing anything that makes you feel happy. Progressing all of the different bottles helps to ensure balance and happiness in the long run. From a slightly longer-term perspective, you might identify you'd like to change career and need some new work experience or study to achieve this. If you're not sure where you're headed, here's an exercise that might help.

Exercise 37: Creating life goals

Imagine yourself looking back at your life from the age of 80 or 100. Whatever feels most relevant and comfortable. Get a large piece of paper and under the following headings, write your answers to the following questions, trying to ignore what you think is expected of you.

- What were your happiest moments?
- What did you learn about yourself?
- What experiences did you have?
- What was your contribution?
- What skills did you acquire?
- What did you enjoy learning?
- What countries did you visit?
- What hobbies did you enjoy?
- Who did you spend time with?
- What talents did you develop?
- What were you grateful for trying?
- How did you best look after yourself physically, emotionally, mentally, spiritually?
- What do you wish you spent more time on/with?

Don't worry if you don't know the answers but keep asking the questions or take steps to find out.

Guided Meditation 12: The Cave of Balance
Use this guided meditation to help you identify and take steps towards creating more balance and peace in your life.

natalieread.online/balance

Summary

○ Building a strong sense of self can increase happiness, decision-making and self-esteem. It also helps us to feel balanced and feel we're working towards something in life.

It also stops us from being affected so much by what others think.

o Understanding your different parts and strengthening the compassionate mediator can help bring about more harmony and balance and a stronger sense of self.

o Having a sense of what's important in life and apportioning time to bring your life into balance can enhance your happiness. Life balance is best with flexibility and flow, so that you allow yourself to be human.

o Taking time for self-reflection and being conscious about taking steps to address happiness and balance is important.

Conclusion

I SEE YOU JUST AS YOU ARE

I wrote this book over a three-year period, although I didn't actually set out to write a book. For a long time, I've felt hugely concerned about the growing mental health problems within young people – the increasing numbers, complexity and the scarcity of resources. I wanted to contribute something positive to help the situation. I looked at lots of different options before deciding to meditate on my next move. Each time I did, I felt compelled to put pen to paper. Before long, I realized I was writing a book. I accepted the challenge with some trepidation. I had no desire to put myself into such a public arena but every time I spoke to people about it, I was inspired by the level of interest. Every time my critic surfaced, my passion to do something – no matter how small – kept me going. Just as I thought I'd finished writing, I had a strong urge to end with the following:

I see you just as you are.

I see you with your amazing qualities. If you don't know yet what I'm talking about, you haven't yet explored yourself enough.

I see you with your flaws and imperfections. I see your humanness. I don't need to turn away from this as I see my own flaws and imperfections too.

I see your beauty. I don't care what you actually look like. I'm speaking about your essence. Who you truly are.

I admire your courage and strength to keep going when you've had a bad day or you're going through something tough.

I might not like your truth sometimes but I admire your willingness to speak it and I grow to respect your authenticity.

Mostly I love your humanness. You're human just like me.

My biggest hope is that you've taken something from this book, no matter how small, and you're now feeling more human and accepting of yourself. I sincerely wish you all the very best for the future. Remember to believe in the uniqueness and beauty of yourself even when there are times when it is hard to do this. Good luck from my heart!

References

Introduction

1. https://www.mind.org.uk/information-support/types-of-mental-health-problems/statistics-and-facts-about-mental-health/how-common-are-mental-health-problems/#. XL7rHf7sbcs; accessed 2 May 2019
2. Institute for Public Policy Research, as quoted in *The Independent*, February 2018
3. NHS Digital report, 'Mental Health of Children and Young People in England', 2017 [PAS]
4. https://www.mentalhealth.org.uk/statistics/mental-health-statistics-children-and-young-people; accessed 2 May 2019
5. https://www.counselling-directory.org.uk/young-people-stats.html; accessed 2 May 2019
6. HRH the Dalai Lama, 'The Paradox of Our Age; www.theartofancientwisdom.com; accessed 2 May 2019
7. Durlosfsky, P. and Bamford, B. quoted in an article by the Mental Health Foundation; https://www.mentalhealth.org.uk/blog/social-media-and-young-peoples-mental-health; accessed 2 May 2019
8. Survey by the Royal Society for Public Health (RSPH) and the Young Health Movement quoted by the BBC news on the NHS website. Https://www.nhs.uk/news/food-and-diet/instagram-ranked-worst-for-mental-health-in-teen-survey/, article dated 19 May 2017
9. https://www.theguardian.com/society/2018/nov/22/why-do-more-young-people-have-mental-health-problems; accessed 2 May 2019

10. All of the guided meditations have been written by me. My influences have come through my training in psychosynthesis, the Diana Cooper Foundation and working with Daniel Mitel and Eloise Bennett. Guided Meditation 10, Body Awareness Scan, in Chapter 13 is inspired by the dis-identification exercise originating from Roberto Assagioli. Guided Meditation 6, Loving Kindness, in Chapter 9 is based on the famous loving-kindness meditation of which there are many versions that can be found freely on the Internet.

Chapter 1

1. This exercise is inspired by a psychosynthesis perspective and from my spiritual trainings.
2. Jeffers, S. *End the Struggle and Dance with Life – How to Build Yourself Up When the World Gets You Down* (Hodder Mobius, 1996)
3. Based on an exercise I learned while training in psychosynthesis.

Chapter 2

1. Brown, B. TED talk 'The Power of vulnerability', 3 April 2017 and Brown, B. (2015)
2. Brown, B. *Daring Greatly: How the Courage to Be Vulnerable Transforms the Way We Live, Love*, Parent and Lead (Penguin Life, 2013)

Chapter 3

1. Some of the ideas in this chapter were inspired by working with Daniel Mitel. Collecting evidance, Exercise 6 and the preceding challenging evidence questions are influenced by CBT (cognitive behavioural therapy) and NLP (neuro linguistic programming). CBT was founded by Aaron Beck and NLP by Richard Bandler and John Grinder.

Chapter 4

1. Brené Brown discusses the work of Dr Linda Hartling in three responses to shame from 'Gifts of Imperfection': https://www. habitsforwellbeing.com/our-responses-to-shame/; accessed 2 May 2019
2. Cooper, D. *Transform Your Life: A Step-by-Step Programme for Change* (Piatkus, 1993)

Chapter 5

1. https://www.mind.org.uk/information-support/tips-for-everyday-living/nature-and-mental-health/#.XMBepP7sbcs; accessed 2 May 2019
2. https://www.health.harvard.edu/mind-and-mood/sour-mood-getting-you-down-get-back-to-nature; accessed 2 May 2019
3. https://www.businessinsider.com/why-spending-more-time-outside-is-healthy-2017-7?r=US&IR=T; accessed 2 May 2019
4. https://www.theguardian.com/society/2017/mar/21/access-nature-reduces-depression-obesity-european-report; accessed 2 May 2019

Chapter 6

1. Whitmore, D. *Psychosynthesis Counselling in Action* (Sage Publications, 2004)
2. Based on a process we used in my psychosynthesis counselling training.

Chapter 7

1. I have been researching self-esteem for a number of years and been influenced by many websites and books, Melanie Fennell and an article by Christine Webber were particularly influential: https://www.netdoctor.co.uk/healthy-living/sex-life/a2308/self-esteem/

2. Based on a process we used in psychosynthesis counselling training.
3. Based on an exercise I learned while training in psychosynthesis.

Chapter 9

1. Harriet Lerner, John Gottman, David Emerald and Diana Cooper among others talk about the 'dynamics at play' within relationships.
2. Harvey, J. 'The Abilene Paradox: The Management of Agreement', 1974; https://en.wikipedia.org/wiki/Abilene_paradox; accessed 2 May 2019
3. https://emmaseppala.com/18-science-based-reasons-try-loving-kindness-meditation-today/; accessed 2 May 2019

Chapter 10

1. I have been running a number of resilience-based workshops for a number of years. Most of my research has come from articles. Some useful references to articles include: https://www.psychologytoday.com/gb/blog/design-your-path/201305/10-traits-emotionally-resilient-people; https://startupbros.com/21-ways-overcome-impostor-syndrome/; https://www.mind.org.uk/search-results?q=developing%20resilience; https://greatergood.berkeley.edu/article/item/five_science_backed_strategies_to_build_resilience
2. Based on the 'Grow Model' which I learned while working with Performance Consultants.

Chapter 11

1. Leadership: 'An Art of Possibility', corporate video ' How to give an A'; https://www.youtu.be/qTKEBygQicO; accessed 2 May 2019

2. https://scienceblogs.com/thepumphandle/2015/02/06/study-self-affirmation-targets-the-brain-in-way-that-makes-us-receptive-to-health-messaging; accessed 2 May 2019

3. https://www.psychologicalscience.org/news/releases/self-affirmation-enhances-performance-makes-us-receptive-to-our-mistakes.html; accessed 2 May 2019

4. Emoto, M. *The Hidden Messages in Water* (Simon and Schuster, 2005)

5. https://www.psychologytoday.com/gb/articles/200306/our-brains-negative-bias; accessed 2 May 2019

6. https://positivepsychologyprogram.com/gratitude-appreciation/, https://www.mindful.org/gratitude-changes-brain/; accessed 2 May 2019

Chapter 12

1. Hahn, T. *True Love – A Practice for Awakening the Heart* (Shambala Publications, 1997)

2. Hartmann, T. *The Last Hours of Ancient Sunlight – The Fate of the World and What We Can Do Before It's Too Late* (Three Rivers Press, 2004)

3. Shapiro, D. *Your Body Speaks Your Mind – Understand How Your Thoughts and Emotions Affect Your Health* (Piatakus, 1996)

Chapter 13

1. Mindfulness has many origins but Jon Kabat Zinn, who founded the Mindfulness-Based Stress Reduction programme in 1979, brought these principles into the mainstream. I have been running mindfulness groups for a number of years and learnt incredible amounts from my colleagues alongside reading and my own spiritual practice and trainings, which are hugely complimentary to mindfulness.

2. Influenced by an exercise I experienced when training with Performance Consultants.

Chapter 14

1. Based on a process we used in psychosynthesis counselling training.
2. The self-compassionate mediator is based on concepts from psychosynthesis, mindfulness and my spiritual trainings.

Bibliography

Assagioli, R. (2007) *Transpersonal Development: The Dimension Beyond Psychosynthesis*, Smiling Wisdom

———————— (2002) *The Act of Will: A Guide to Self-actualization and Self-realization*, Psychosynthesis and Education Trust

Bandhu, M. (2009) *Life with Full Attention: A Practical Course in Mindfulness*, Windhorse publications

Brown, B. (2015) *Daring Greatly: How the Courage to Be Vulnerable Transforms the Way We Live*, Love, Parent and Lead, Penguin Life.

Cooper, D. (2000) *A Little Light on the Spiritual Laws*, Hodder and Stoughton

———————— (2012) *Transform Your Life*, Piatkus

———————— (2004) *A New Light on Ascension*, Findhorn Press

Emerald, D. (2010) *The Power of TED*: The Empowerment Dynamic, Polaris Publishing

Feldman, C. (1998) *Meditation Plain and Simple*, Element

Fennel, M. (2009) *Overcoming Low Self-esteem: A Self-help Guide Using CBT*, Basic Books

Ferrucci, P. (2004) *What We May Be*, Penguin

Firman, J. and Gila, A. (1997) *The Primal Wound: A Transpersonal View of Trauma, Addiction and Growth*, State University of New York Press

Gottman, J. and Silver, N. (2015) *The 7 Principles for Making Marriage Work*, Harmony books

Hartmann, T. (2004) The Last Hours of Ancient Sunlight: The Fate of the World and What We Can Do Before It's Too Late, Three Rivers Press

Huber, C. (1999) *The Depression Book: Depression as an Opportunity for Spiritual Growth*, Keep It Simple Books

Jeffers, S. (1996) *End the Struggle and Dance with Life: How to Build Yourself Up When the World Gets You Down*, Hodder Mobius

Jenkins, H. and Fennel, M. (2004) *Building Self-Esteem*, Oxford Cognitive Therapy Centre

Lama, D. and Cutler, C.H. (1998) *The Art of Happiness: A Handbook for Living*, Coronet books

Lerner, H. (2004) *The Dance of Anger*, Element

Kennerley, H. (2017) *Managing Anxiety: A User's Manual*, Oxford Cognitive Therapy Centre

Myss, C. (1997) *Why People Don't Heal and How They Can: A Practical Programme for Healing Body*, Mind and Spirit, Bantam

Mitel, D. (2015) *This Now Is Eternity: 21 Ancient Meditations for Awakening to Whom You Really Are*, Balboa Press

Padesky, C. and Mooney, K. (2012) 'Strengths-based Cognitive Behavioural Therapy: A 4-step Model to Build Resilience', *Clinical Psychology and Psychotherapy*

Rouf, K. (2013) *Keep Safe and Carry On: Coping with Suicidal Feelings*, Oxford Cognitive Therapy Centre

Shapiro, D. (1996) *Your Body Speaks Your Mind*, Piatkus

Stone, J.D. (1999) *Soul Psychology*, Ballantine Wellspring

Thich Nhat H. (2004) *True Love: A Practice for Awakening the Heart*, Shambala Publications

Whitmore, D. (2004) *Psychosynthesis Counselling in Action*, Sage Publications

Whitmore, J. (2002) *Coaching for Performance*, Nicolas Brealey Publishing.

William, A. (2015) *Medical Medium: Secrets Behind Chronic and Mystery Illness and How to Finally Heal*, Hay House

Williams, M. and Penman, D. (2011) *Mindfulness: A Practical Guide to Finding Peace in a Frantic World*, Piatkus

Yeomans, T. (unknown) 'Psychosynthesis Exercises for Personal and Spiritual Growth', an article posted on Psychosynthesis Trust website; https://psychosynthesistrust.org.uk/psychosynthesis-exercises-for-personal-spiritual-growth/

TED Talks

Brown, B. 'The Power of Vulnerability' - 3 April 2017, 'Listening to Shame', 11 March 2014

Rankin, L. 'The Shocking Truth About Your Health', 6 December 2011

Appendix I

LIST OF GUIDED MEDITATIONS

All of the meditations/visualizations are beneficial in different ways and can be used to suit any presenting issue. I have made suggestions in each chapter although they can be used more generally than this. If you like a particular one and it resonates, using it regularly will bring the most benefit. Please refer back to the introduction for more information about meditations and how to use them.

Guided Meditation 1: The Crossroad (Chapter 1 – Going with the Flow of Life): natalieread.online/crossroad

Guided Meditation 2: The Beach (Chapter 2 – Emotions – Friend or Foe?): natalieread.online/beach

Guided Meditation 3: Weeding Your Garden (Chapter 3 – Life Is a Story): natalieread.online/garden

Guided Meditation 4: The Healing Flame (Chapter 5 – Overcoming Depression and Low Mood): natalieread.online/flame

Guided Meditation 5: The Seed (Chapter 7 – Building Self-Esteem): natalieread.online/seed

Guided Meditation 6: Loving Kindness (Chapter 9 – Improving Relationships with Others): natalieread.online/kindness

Guided Meditation 7: The Tree (Chapter 10 – Building Resilience to Overcome Difficulties): natalieread.online/tree

Guided Meditation 8: The island (Chapter 11 – Writing New Positive Chapters and Stories): natalieread.online/island

Guided Meditation 9: Unconditional Love (Chapter 12 – Path to Self-love): natalieread.online/love

Guided Meditation 10: Body Awareness Scan (Chapter 13 – Embracing Peace): natalieread.online/scan

Guided Meditation 11: Focusing on Positive Qualities (Chapter 13 – Embracing Peace): natalieread.online/focus

Guided Meditation 12: The Cave of Balance (Chapter 14 – Strengthening Identity and Balance): natalieread.online/balance

Appendix II

LIST OF
EXERCISES

All of the exercises have been written to complement the material in each chapter. It might be helpful to record your reflections in a journal as you may find you want to refer back to a previous exercise or update your answers over time.

Exercise 1: Building resilience (Chapter 1 – Going with the Flow of Life)

Exercise 2: Understanding what's important (Chapter 1 – Going with the Flow of Life)

Exercise 3: Understanding your thoughts and feelings (Chapter 2 – Emotions – Friend or Foe?)

Exercise 4: Understanding your stories and beliefs (Chapter 3 – Life Is a Story)

Exercise 5: Seeing the impact of your beliefs (Chapter 3 – Life Is a Story)

Exercise 6: Challenging your story (Chapter 3 – Life Is a Story)

Exercise 7: Reframing (Chapter 3 – Life Is a Story)

Exercise 8: Understanding your relationships (Chapter 4 – Understanding Relationships)

Exercise 9: Deep breath (Chapter 6 – Reducing Anxiety)

Exercise 10: Overcoming panic breath (Chapter 6 – Reducing Anxiety)

Exercise 11: Helping anxiety do its job (Chapter 6 – Reducing Anxiety)

Exercise 12: Understanding the anxious part of you (Chapter 6 – Reducing Anxiety)

Exercise 13: Understanding your self-esteem (Chapter 7 – Building Self-esteem)

Exercise 14: Identify alternative interpretations (Chapter 7 – Building Self-esteem)

Exercise 15: Understanding the critic (Chapter 7 – Building Self-esteem)

Exercise 16: Initiate a positive cycle of feedback (Chapter 7 – Building Self-esteem)

Exercise 17: Body gratitude (Chapter 7 – Building Self-esteem)

Exercise 18: Looking for positives (Chapter 7 – Building Self-esteem)

Exercise 19: Making decisions (Chapter 7 – Building Self-esteem)

Exercise 20: Working with the block (Chapter 7 – Building Self-esteem)

LIST OF EXERCISES

Exercise 21: Understanding your anger (Chapter 8 – Managing Anger)

Exercise 22: Evaluate your level of resilience (Chapter 10 – Building Resilience to Overcome Difficulties)

Exercise 23: Self-care questionnaire (Chapter 10 – Building Resilience to Overcome Difficulties)

Exercise 24: Finding a way forwards (Chapter 10 – Building Resilience to Overcome Difficulties)

Exercise 25: Using affirmations (Chapter 11 – Writing New Positive Chapters and Stories)

Exercise 26: Creating positive stories (Chapter 11 – Writing New Positive Chapters and Stories)

Exercise 27: Daily gratitude (Chapter 11 – Writing New Positive Chapters and Stories)

Exercise 28: Sending unconditional love (Chapter 12 – Path to Self)

Exercise 29: Forgiveness and letting go (Chapter 12 – Path to Self)

Exercise 30: Performance – sports and hobbies (Chapter 13 – Embracing Peace)

Exercise 31: Performance – writing and creating (Chapter 13 – Embracing Peace)

Exercise 32: Turning worry into a positive scenario (Chapter 13 – Embracing Peace)

Exercise 33: Your values (Chapter 14 – Strengthening Identity and Balance)

Exercise 34: Understanding your parts (Chapter 14 – Strengthening Identity and Balance)

Exercise 35: Walking in nature (Chapter 14 – Strengthening Identity and Balance)

Exercise 36: Life-balance audit (Chapter 14 – Strengthening Identity and Balance)

Exercise 37: Creating life goals (Chapter 14 – Strengthening Identity and Balance)

Resources

Here follows a list of resources you might find helpful, but do discern which might be the most appropriate for you. You may also like to read some of the titles listed in the Bibliography.

In the meantime, if you're in crisis or at risk of harm remember:

- Contact your doctor or medical practitioner as your first port of call. If they are closed, there may be an out of hours service. If you are concerned about your level of safety and it's an emergency, please contact your nearest emergency department.
- Call the Samaritans on 08457 90 90 90 to talk to a trained volunteer. (Available in other countries. Please check local number)

Counselling

To find a counsellor, contact your doctor, university or employer website or find one direct by checking for local services on the Internet. Alternatively, search for one of the following organizations to find a private counsellor near you.

www.BACP.co.uk

www.UKCP.co.uk

For more about psychosynthesis:
https://psychosynthesistrust.org.uk/

General self-help

Action for Happiness: Promotes positive psychology and happiness – the Dalai Lama is one of the charity's patrons: https://www.actionforhappiness.org/

CBT: Provides an information sheet on problem-solving, distorted thinking habits and information on a wide variety of mental health topics: www.getselfhelp.co.uk

Mind: A mental health charity with articles, self-help guides and helpline numbers: www.mind.org.uk

Mood Juice: Self-help guides: https://www.moodjuice.scot.nhs.uk/

Papyrus: A voluntary organization supporting teenagers and young adults in the prevention of suicide: https://papyrus-uk.org/

Rethink Mental Illness: Fact sheets, membership and how to find support in your area: Https://www.rethink.org/

USA specific resources:

Mental Health America: Screening tools and access to local support programs: https://www.mentalhealthamerica.net

National Alliance on Mental Health: Crisis helpline, blogs and how to find support in your specific state including student specific groups: https://www.nami.org

The Child Mind Institute: Support for children and families. Access to treatments, information and guidance, online resources: https://www.childmind.org

Self-esteem

Dove Campaign for Real Beauty: https://www.dove.com/uk/
stories/campaigns.html

Esteem: Volunteering and mentoring opportunities for 14–26-year-
olds: http://esteem.org.uk/

Enlightenment Portal: Offers 15 self-esteem building
opportunities for children and adults: https://enlightenmentportal.
com/development/self-esteem-building-activities/

MIND: https://www.mind.org.uk/media/715750/how-to-increase-
your-self-esteem-2013.pdf

National Association for Healthy Self-esteem: http://
healthyselfesteem.org/

Psychology Today: https://www.psychologytoday.com/us/blog/
hide-and-seek/201205/building-confidence-and-self-esteem

Self-compassion: www.selfcompassion.org

Depression and low mood

Healthline: Article with information about apps that can help
depression: https://www.healthline.com/health/depression/top-
iphone-android-apps

Help Guide: Information and tips to overcome depression and
low mood: https://www.helpguide.org/articles/depression/coping-
with-depression.htm

Mood Gym-interactive Program: Five modules based on cognitive behavioural therapy and interpersonal therapy designed to help young adults: http://healthyyoungmindspennine.nhs.uk/resource-centre/apps/moodgym/

Students Against Depression: A website for students who are depressed, anxious, have low mood or are having suicidal thoughts. http://studentsagainstdepression.org/

Anxiety

Anxiety: A national charity offering information, self-help sheets about various different types of anxiety and access to therapeutic support: https://www.anxietyuk.org.uk/

The Mental Health Foundation: Offers information and support for overcoming anxiety and fear: https://www.mentalhealth.org.uk/publications/overcome-fear-anxiety/

No More Panic: Information about anxiety, phobias, panic and OCD, as well as articles, self-help information and an online chatroom: https://www.nomorepanic.co.uk/

Students Against Depression: For students who are depressed, anxious, have low mood or are having suicidal thoughts: http://studentsagainstdepression.org/

This Way Up: Article about 12 different free apps that help with stress and anxiety: https://thiswayup.org.au/12-free-apps-to-help-you-beat-stress/

Young Minds: Information about anxiety and where to get help: https://youngminds.org.uk/find-help/conditions/anxiety/

Anger

British Association of Anger Management: Information, a free self-assessment test and access to courses: www.angermanage. co.uk

MIND: Charity offering information and tips: https://www.mind.org.uk/information-support/types-of-mental-health-problems/anger/#.XJDVi_5Cfcs

Mood Juice: Self-help guide: https://www.moodjuice.scot.nhs.uk/anger.asp

NHS: Tips on managing anger and how to seek help: https://www.nhs.uk/conditions/stress-anxiety-depression/controlling-anger/

Think Simple Now: Article on 15 tips to improve anger: http://thinksimplenow.com/happiness/15-simple-ways-to-overcome-anger/

Bereavement

Care for the Family: Bereavement support for all different types of loss: https://www.careforthefamily.org.uk/family-life/bereavement-support

Child Bereavement UK: App and information for 11–25-year-olds: https://childbereavementuk.org/Our App/

Cruse: National bereavement charity offering information and how to get support: https://www.cruse.org.uk/

Support After Suicide: Support for anyone affected by suicide: http://supportaftersuicide.org.uk/emotional-support/

Addictions

Down Your Drink: Support to help reduce alcohol consumption: https://www.downyourdrink.org.uk/

Drug Wise: Evidence-based information on drugs, alcohol and tobacco: https://www.drugwise.org.uk/

Frank: Information about drugs: https://www.talktofrank.com/

NHS: Information about drinking: https://www.nhs.uk/live-well/alcohol-support/

Self Help for Substance Abuse: https://www.getselfhelp.co.uk/substancemisuse.htm

It's the Drink Talking: Youth blog about drinking: http://www.itsthedrinktalking.co.uk/

Self-harm

Harmless: User-led charity providing support: http://www.harmless.org.uk/

Mind: Resources for self-harm: https://www.mind.org.uk/information-support/types-of-mental-health-problems/self-harm/#.XK3psv7sbcs

Selfharm UK: Dedicated to self-harm recovery, insight and support: https://www.selfharm.co.uk/

The Mix: Information about strategies to prevent self-harm: https://www.themix.org.uk/mental-health/self-harm

Sex and relationships

Asexuality: Information on asexuality: https://www.asexuality.org/

BISH: Sex and relationships help for all genders and sexualities: https://www.bishuk.com/

Love Is Respect: Information about healthy relationships: https://www.loveisrespect.org/healthy-relationships/

Gottman Institute: Video on four styles of communication that can lead to relationship breakdown: https://www.youtube.com/watch?v=1o30Ps-_8is

NHS: Advice on sexual relationships: https://www.nhs.uk/live-well/sexual-health/15-things-young-people-should-know-about-sex/

Professional Counselling: Support and advice on relationships: https://www.professional-counselling.com/

Psychology Today: Article on healthy relationships: https://www.psychologytoday.com/us/blog/in-practice/201301/50-characteristics-healthy-relationships

The Mix: Information about sexuality and relationships: https://www.themix.org.uk/sex-and-relationships

Rape and sexual violence

Domestic Abuse: Information and helpline for women: https://domestic-abuse.org/?src=tcu21&msclkid=34c51390a5fd1aafabdb4f3d485bf4e1

Galop: LGBT+ anti-violence charity to support anyone LGBT who has experienced hate crime, domestic violence or sexual violence: http://www.galop.org.uk/domesticabuse/

NSPCC: Information about domestic and child abuse: https://www.nspcc.org.uk/preventing-abuse/child-abuse-and-neglect/domestic-abuse/

Pennyline: Domestic abuse support: https://domestic-abuse.org/?src=tcu21&msclkid=34c51390a5fd1aafabdb4f3d485bf4e1

Rape Crisis: England and Wales: https://rapecrisis.org.uk/

Safeline: https://www.safeline.org.uk/

The Survivors Trust: Support and information for anyone affected by sexual violence and rape: https://thesurvivorstrust.org/

Social media and mental health

The Mental Health Foundation: Information on how mental health is affected by social media use. There are self-help guides, as well as links to 'Ditch the Label', an anti-bullying charity, and Aye Mind, which helps to improve mental health through positive social media: https://www.mentalhealth.org.uk/blog/social-media-and-young-peoples-mental-health

Mindfulness and relaxation

Buddhify: App for mindfulness and meditation: buddhify.com

Calm: Meditations and sleep stories to improve sleep, anxiety and relaxation: calm.com

Frantic World: Advice on finding peace with information and free meditations: http://franticworld.com/free-meditations-from-mindfulness/

Headspace: Meditation app (free and subscription) with lots of information and meditations: headspace.com

Acknowledgements

I'm grateful to all the people I've ever come into contact with and all the life experiences I've had; they have all helped me prepare the stage for this book.

Underpinning the foundations of my work is my training in Psychosynthesis Counselling. Roberto Assagioli trained alongside Sigmund Freud and Carl Jung before branching off to establish Psychosynthesis. Assagioli drew upon many Eastern traditions and created a transpersonal approach working with the mind, body and spirit. I am indebted to all the wonderful teachers and peers I met during my training at the Psychosynthesis Trust.

I have incorporated aspects of CBT, mindfulness, and body and trauma work into my working model, which I have learned through a breadth of workshops, reading and working with my colleagues. I am particularly grateful to Carmen Alfonso, Dave Sibley, Glenn Mower and Ro Bolland who I have worked alongside in either Resilience, Self-Esteem or Mindfulness programmes – I have learnt so much from each of you. I am also grateful to Eliza Aspinall who ran a training day on body dysmorphia which moved me so much, inspired exercise 17 and motivated me to keep going with this book. I am extremely grateful to all of my colleagues in Student Counselling. I admire your dedication and passion to the work that you do.

I thank all of the amazing and courageous clients that I've worked with over the years, both in a student counselling or private setting. Each of you holds a special place in my heart and I sincerely wish you well.

ACKNOWLEDGEMENTS

I spent 13 years in the corporate sector and I bring my knowledge of organizational culture, coaching, personal and leadership development to my work. I trained in coaching, business NLP and executive coaching with R&A, Performance Consultants and Lee Hecht Harrison. I'm also grateful to Jonathan Brown, Nikki Mansell Rogers, Andrea Cooper and Chantal Misquitta for the information about Roger Bannister and introducing me to the Ben Zander video. Thank you to Guy Marriot for asking me many questions over 20 years ago; this was the inspiration for Exercise 37 on setting goals.

My deepest gratitude to my teachers Eloise Bennett and Daniel Mitel who I've worked with over a number of years. I've trained in ascension (Diana Cooper Foundation), heart imagery, meditation in the tiny space of the heart and kriya yoga, plus numerous other things over the years. You have inspired and mentored me and it's an honour to call you friends. Also special thanks to everybody who I crossed paths with at Ginger Hill on retreat. There's too many to mention but you know who you are and I'm eternally grateful. All of this training plus extensive reading in many more areas has influenced many ideas in this book.

I've been lucky enough to have many different friends over the years all of which have supported me and made life interesting in so many ways. I wish I could mention you all. I am particularly grateful to the friends who were there during the start of my conscious journey early in my twenties and who still support me today - Karen Higgins, Jo McClements, Maria Farrow, Cali White and Simone Ford. Also, thank you to Louise Caine who listens to me on a weekly basis! And to all my friends, I'm very grateful to you all.

In helping me with this book, huge thanks to Geraldine Taylor, Eliza Aspinall, Glenn Mower, Jane Blackhurst, Vicky Lacey, Kendra Futcher, Adrian Read and Sarah Moore for reading and providing invaluable feedback on this manuscript at various stages of its evolution. Your kindness and valuable insight was very much appreciated. Special thanks to the generosity of Carmen Alfonso who read the entire thing and inspired me to keep going.

Huge gratitude to Sandy Draper whose support and encouragement while editing this book has been hugely helpful. Also to the team at I AM self-publishing for all their advice, encouragement and help in making this book a reality.

Finally, I am so grateful to my family who've always been there for me. I am so blessed to have you all. Again too many to mention but special thanks to Adrian for his unconditional support and love – I couldn't do this without you. To my amazing parents Sarah, Colin, Barry and Claire. And to Maia and Annabel who inspire me every day and whose generation I hope will benefit from this book.

About the Author

Natalie Read is a BACP accredited counsellor (Psychosynthesis Counselling – PG dip) with an additional degree in Business Studies (BA Hons). She has worked as a counsellor within a University Student Counselling Service for over 12 years. During this time she has worked with clients in a one-to-one capacity as well as running workshops and groups. She has a particular passion and experience in running self-esteem, resilience, mindfulness and meditation groups. Prior to this Natalie worked for 10 years in a major global corporate company in Sales, Marketing and HR and also had a number of consultancy roles whilst training to be a counsellor. During this time, she was involved in organizational culture change, coaching and leadership programs.

Natalie is passionate about helping people to find peace and happiness in their life and has explored many different approaches to do so. For over 20 years, she has followed a spiritual quest to find peace and happiness in herself. She brings all of this information blended with her own counselling and coaching experience in this book. Natalie has been incorporating this blended approach for many years in private workshops and groups.

Natalie is passionate about looking after people and this planet. She wholeheartedly believes in the importance of helping people towards self-awareness, self-acceptance and self-love in order to obtain long-lasting and fundamental change. Through this book she hopes to contribute towards helping to address the growing mental health crisis.

Printed in Great Britain
by Amazon

36043047R00152